*Silver Burdett Picture Histories*

# Life in Ancient Greece

Pierre Miquel
Illustrated by Pierre Probst

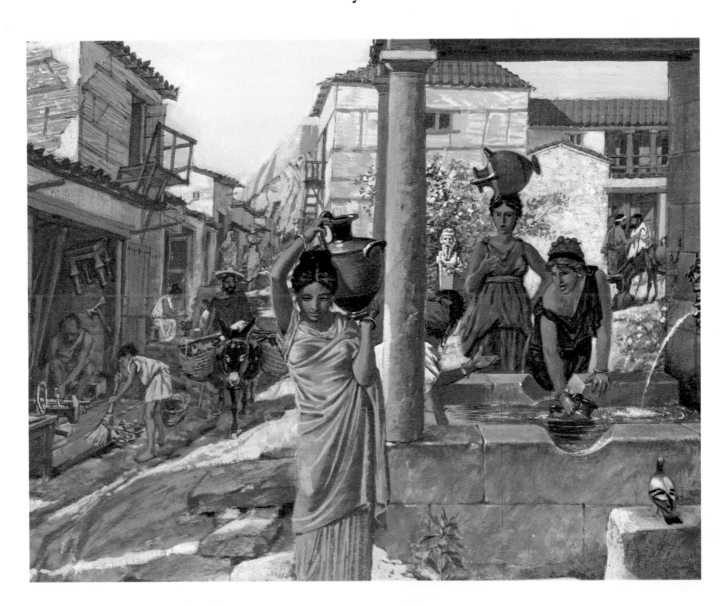

**Library of Congress Cataloging in Publication Data**

Miquel, Pierre, 1930–
  Life in ancient Greece.

  (Silver Burdett picture histories)
  Translation of: Au temps de la Grèce ancienne.
  Includes index.
  Summary: Depicts the civilization of ancient Greece,
including its economy, food, crafts, family rituals,
culture, and military techniques.
  1. Greece—Civilization—To 146 B.C.—Juvenile
literature. [1. Greece—Civilization—To 146 B.C.]
I. Title. II. Probst, Pierre, 1913-    ill.
III. Series.
DF77.Mo413  1985       938        85-40209

ISBN 0-382-09085-3
ISBN 0-382-06887-4 (lib. bdg.)


Translated and adapted by Anthea Ridett
from La Vie privée des Hommes: Au temps de la Grèce ancienne.
First published in France in 1981 by
Librairie Hachette, Paris

# Contents

| | Page |
|---|---|
| The Greeks and their Ancestors | 4 |
| At the Mercy of the Winds | 10 |
| Mining and Money | 12 |
| Wheat, Honey, and Olives | 14 |
| Life in Fifth-Century Athens | 16 |
| Trading in the Agora | 18 |
| Crafts and Public Works | 20 |
| Artists of Rare Talent | 22 |
| Democracy and Citizenship | 24 |
| Family Rituals | 26 |
| Life at Home | 28 |
| Grammatists, Doctors, and Philosophers | 30 |
| Fun and Games | 32 |
| The Greek Theater | 34 |
| Sporting Events | 36 |
| The Importance of Architecture | 38 |
| Ready for War | 40 |
| Military Techniques | 42 |
| On the Battlefield | 44 |
| Warships | 46 |
| The Power of the Gods | 48 |
| Religious Festivals | 50 |
| Temples and Sanctuaries | 52 |
| Gods and Goddesses | 54 |
| The Animals of Ancient Greece | 56 |
| An Imaginary Letter | 56 |
| Donkeys, Mules, and Horses | 60 |
| Fish and Meat in Greek Meals | 61 |
| Did You Know? | 62 |
| Glossary | 63 |
| Index | 64 |

# The Greeks And Their Ancestors

ASS. G. BUDÉ

In ancient times the quickest and safest way to travel from one place in Greece to another was by boat. For the landscape of Greece consists of a complicated series of mountain ridges, separating small plains and valleys that are connected only by narrow passes. Some mountain peaks, like Parnassus and Olympus, are over 8,000 feet high, plunging steeply down to the Aegean Sea.

In the old days, a traveler going from north to south would see many different kinds of landscape. In the north was the three-pronged, mountainous peninsula of Chalcidice. On one side lay the mountains of Thrace, running from the east to the Bosporus strait and the Hellespont (now the Dardanelles). To the west lay the fertile plain of Macedonia, where horses peacefully grazed in the lush grass. Between Macedonia and the rich, wheat-growing plain of Thessaly farther south, lay the solid mountain ridge of Olympus, barring the main road from invaders. The diagonal fold of the Pindus mountains to the west divided Thessaly from the craggy region of Epirus.

From the north, a traveler had to cross the narrow pass of Thermopylae to reach the nome or region of Boeotia, with its city of Thebes and the nome of Attica, with its capital of Athens. To get to Delphi, seat of the famous oracle, one had to cross the Parnassus mountains. Finally, the Corinth Isthmus had to be crossed to reach the mountainous peninsula of the Peloponnesus, with its many great cities—Corinth in the north, Olympia to the west, Sparta in the south, and Mycenae, Argos, and Epidaurus to the east.

The Greek islands, then as now, were even more varied: some of them huge, like enormous landmarks in the Aegean Sea—Crete and Rhodes, which close the sea to the south, and Samothrace, Lemnos, and Lesbos, the last stopping points before one reached the straits of the Black Sea.

Around mainland Greece itself the sea is studded with islands, including Corfu and Ithaca to the west and Euboea to the east. The Aegean is dotted with archipelagos (chains of mountainous islands)—the Northern and Southern Sporades and between them the Cyclades.

## The First Greeks

With 2,000 miles of coastline, the people of Greece were seafarers rather than farmers, although they did cultivate all the land they could. Wheat, vines, and olives flourished in the sunny climate. Around 2000 B.C. (when the Egyptian civilization was 1,000 years old) a race of people had moved onto the peninsula, probably from the plains of southern Russia. They came in small successive waves with their wives, children, and herds. They were Aryans, or Indo-Europeans, like the Persians and Hittites. They occupied the land and built villages which later grew into fortified towns.

These early Greeks, who populated the valleys and islands between 2000 and 1200 B.C., were called *Achaeans*. They chose to settle mainly on the hills and slopes of the Peloponnesus. Traces of their civilization have been found at Mycenae and also near Tiryns and Argos. They traveled south, too. Around 1400 B.C. they invaded the island of Crete, which already had its own people and culture.

These early Greeks were sailors, as well as shepherds and goatherds. They built lightweight, easily manageable boats in which they traveled east. They were soon to be found on the Aegean islands and the coast of Asia Minor, where they beseiged and captured the city of Troy, probably around 1200 B.C. Their warriors were led by chieftains called "kings." They had chariots, bronze weapons, and armor, and they built massive stone forts. They worshiped gods and buried their dead in huge tombs. Traces of their writing have been found. The Achaeans, these early Greeks, had a true civilization, known as the Mycenaean civilization.

Around 1200 B.C. they were driven out by a great wave of new invaders, the Dorians who came from the borders of the Danube in the north. They followed exactly the same route as their predecessors. They fought and pillaged, using iron weapons. They captured and destroyed the Achaean cities, built cities of their own, and fought among themselves. They also developed sea trade with the islands, and they adopted the traditions and religion of the Achaeans. So a fusion came about between the old inhabitants of Greece and the new.

HACHETTE BN

Athenian currency

*A drachma was made of 4.36 grams of silver. There were coins worth one, two, four and ten drachmas.*

*The drachma was divided into smaller coins, called obols: 6 obols = one drachma.*

*The obol was divided into the half-obol (diobol, worth one-third of a drachma) and into three-quarters (the tritemorion), one quarter (tetratemorion) and one eighth (hemitetratemorion).*

*Two units were not coins but measures of silver weight; they were:*

*The mina, worth 100 drachmas.*
*The talent, worth 60 minas, or 6000 drachmas.*

Socrate

ΠΕΡΙΚΛΗΣ
ΞΑΝΘΙΠΠΟΥ
ΑΘΗΝΑΙΟΣ

Périclès

> **Important people**
>
> *Philosophers:*
> Socrates, Plato, and Aristotle
> *Architects:*
> Phidias, Mnesicles, and Hippodamus
> of Miletus
> *Playwrights:*
> Aeschylus, Sophocles, Euripides
> (tragedy), and Aristophanes (comedy)
> *Sculptors:*
> Phidias, Praxiteles, and Scopas
> *Generals:*
> Themistocles, Aristeides, and Pericles

> **The Athenian standing army in the time of Pericles:**
>
> *13,000 hoplites (armed troops)*
> *1,000 horsemen*
> *Territorial army of 1,500 ephebes*
> *(young men doing military training) and*
> *9,000 metics (foreigners) with 2,500*
> *veterans guarding the ports and forts*
> *Total: 27,400 armed men*

## The Spread of the Greek Cities

800 to 600 B.C. is known as the Archaic period. During this time independent towns called *city-states* were built everywhere. The most active and powerful cities founded colonies on the coasts of Asia Minor and the Black Sea, and even towards the west on the coasts of southern Italy and Sicily. They spread to the shores of southern Gaul, where the Phocaeans founded Marseilles. In these city-states the same language was spoken, the same gods worshiped, and the same tales told—epic poems like Homer's *Iliad* and *Odyssey*. Greece became a complete world of its own, with a unified way of life and its own way of thought.

One city, however, was different from all the others. That city was Sparta. There all that mattered was physical strength and fighting ability. Sparta was in complete contrast with the seafaring city of Athens. Its port of Piraeus enabled Athens to trade abroad, and the plains of Attica surrounding it made it rich in wheat and olives.

The Greek cities were constantly squabbling among themselves, but in the fifth century B.C. they united against a common threat from Asia. The great Persian king, Darius, and later his son Xerxes captured and occupied the Greek cities in Asia Minor, and then crossed the straits to invade mainland Greece. Athens organized the city-states to form a league against the Persians. The Athenians beat the invaders on land at Marathon, and at sea in the Battle of Salamis. Athens went on to found a great empire stretching from Asia Minor westward. In the fifth century B.C. it was at the height of its power.

Athens, enjoying renewed peace and prosperity, became an extraordinary cultural center from which civilization spread throughout the entire Mediterranean basin. But once the foreign invaders had been vanquished, the city-states began fighting among themselves again. The Peloponnesian War broke out between Athens and Sparta. It lasted twenty-six years with neither side ever really winning or losing. The result was that when another threat loomed, this time from the north, the cities were unable to defend themselves. One after another, they were destroyed.

## Alexander and His Empire

After 338 B.C. the Macedonian kings, Philip and then his son Alexander, conquered the whole of Greece. A new era began for the cities. For two centuries, the fifth and fourth, they had enjoyed a brilliant civilization. Now they had lost their independence and were part of the empire of the young Alexander, the greatest conqueror in the world. Alexander's power extended east as far as the borders of the Persian empire and India. After his death his empire was broken up into independent kingdoms, which made it easy for the Romans to take over from 150 to 30 B.C. Greece became a Roman province, and its culture was absorbed by the Roman Empire.

## The Invention of Democracy

The flowering of Greek independence and prosperity lasted only a short time, for about 150 years between 500 and 338 B.C. But the Greeks had made a totally new and far-reaching contribution to civilization. It is true that, like other races, they had slaves and imposed strict limits on entry to their cities. But Greek citizens were free men, whether they were oarsmen, peasants, or knights. They invented a form of government which was to influence the future of the world—democracy, or government by the people. They elected their magistrates, judges, and generals—the people of Athens carried out their own justice. Their cities had constitutions and laws which no one could violate. And they prized freedom above all.

They studied the collective knowledge of other nations, the Egyptians, Assyrians, and Babylonians, turning it into a coherent whole, and they produced new, original systems of thought. The greatest philosophers and mathematicians of the ancient world were Greeks. The Greeks invented drama and comedy, epic poetry, and oratory. Their sculptors and architects created cities reflecting their culture, with public squares surrounded by colonnades and cemeteries full of sculpted tombs. They paved their roads and built acropolises—citadels where they put up magnificent temples. Greek religion crossed the seas. Apollo was worshiped in Asia and Artemis in Marseilles. For the first time in world history art, science, and philosophy rose above the limitations of everyday life. The Greeks invented the love of humankind and cultivated humanistic values. Their greatest discovery was the respect which people owe to each other.

1230 B.C. or 1225 B.C.: Capture of T
490 B.C.: Athenian victory over the Persians at Marathon.
480 B.C.: Persian victory over King Leonidas at Thermopylae. Naval victory by the Greeks at Salamis.
479 B.C.: Greek victories over the Persians at Platea and Mycale.
406 B.C.: Athenian victory at the Arginusae islands (during the Peloponnesian War between Athens and Sparta).
405 B.C.: Defeat of Athens at Aegospotami (in the Peloponnesian War).
371 B.C.: Victory at Leuctra by the Thebans, led by Epaminondas, against Sparta.
362 B.C.: Spartan victory over Thebes at Mantinea. Death of Epaminondas.
338 B.C.: The Greeks defeated at Chaeronea by Philip, King of Macedonia.

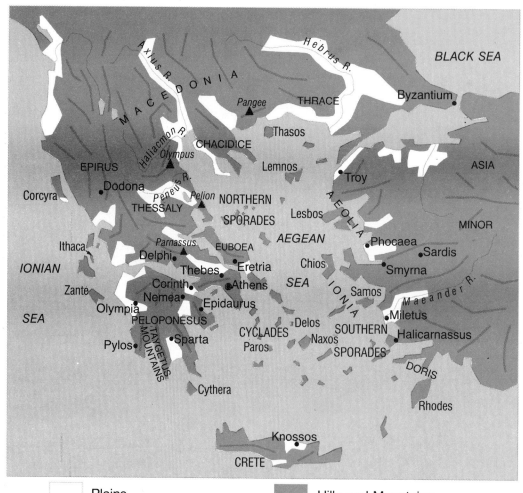

Plains

Hills and Mountains

Greece and the coast of Asia

BLACK SEA

Byzantium

THRACE

*Axius R.*

M A C E D O N I A

*Hebrus R.*

*Pangee* ▲

Thasos

*Haliacmon R.*

CHACIDICE

*Olympus* ▲

EPIRUS

Lemnos

ASIA

Corcyra

Dodona

*Peneus R.*

*Pelion* ▲

Troy

NORTHERN

THESSALY

SPORADES

Lesbos

A E O L I A

MINOR

Ithaca

*Parnassus* ▲

EUBOEA

*AEGEAN*

Phocaea

IONIAN

Delphi

Thebes

Eretria

Chios

Sardis

Zante

Corinth

Athens

*SEA*

Smyrna

*Maeander R.*

Nemea

Epidaurus

Samos

Olympia

PELOPONESUS

Delos

SOUTHERN

Miletus

SEA

TAYGETUS MOUNTAINS

Sparta

CYCLADES

Naxos

SPORADES

Halicarnassus

Pylos

Paros

I O N I A

DORIS

Cythera

Rhodes

Knossos

CRETE

8

# At the Mercy of the Winds

"When you go round Cape Malea," goes a Greek saying, "forget everything you have left at home." Cape Malea is the south-westernmost tip of the Peloponnesus. For a Greek, it was an even greater risk to journey west, towards the "Gates of Hercules" (now the Straits of Gibraltar) than to sail eastward.

In the fifth century B.C. sea travel was still an adventure. It took at least two months to cross the Mediterranean from west to east, traveling along the coastline at speeds averaging between three and five knots. (A knot = 1 nautical mile per hour, approximately 1¹/₇ mile.) Only the boldest navigators sailed directly from Crete to Egypt, a crossing that took five days. Other travelers preferred to trade by sailing along the coast from port to port.

Merchant ships were round and heavy (though never larger than 400 tons), and they moved quite slowly. War galleys, called *triremes*, were less dependent on the wind, since they were powered by oarsmen as well as sails. At the prow the helmsman steered his ship with a hand-held, pivoting oar. He used the stars to guide him at dawn and twilight—for as a general rule

sailors only set out to sea at sunrise, and beached their ships on shore every evening. When there was no wind the oarsmen had to row with all their might, while in rough weather great waves would wash over the decks. In a very heavy storm a ship would have to take shelter and the sailors would have to move quickly to keep their ships from sinking. At certain times of year—like the season of the equinoctial storms—there were a large number of shipwrecks.

Pirates became less and less common, particularly after the famous Athenian fleet was organized to pursue them in their famous triremes the moment they were sighted. This made it safe for merchant ships to set out freely from Piraeus, the port of Athens, or from Corinth or Aegina, to get wheat from Egypt, metals from the Black Sea and slaves from the West.

Setting out to sea at dawn

All the Greeks fished for seafood, using mainly lines, nets, and baskets. They caught shellfish, mollusks, and all kinds of fish that swam around the island shores. People also bought fish in the market, and dried them to preserve them.

At Cyzicus on the Black Sea coast, Greek fishermen would watch for the schools of tunny, sometimes as big as three yards long, weighing over 1500 pounds. They surrounded them with their boats, trapped them in special nets and killed them with harpoons.

The route around the Peloponnesian peninsula from the Aegean to the Ionian was filled with dangers like rocky coasts and pirates. So the Greek sailors linked the two seas by building a wooden road that was later paved. Donkeys or horses hauled the boats across the isthmus. This system saved several days' sailing time. Today the isthmus is crossed by the Corinth Canal.

Merchant ships were slow and heavy, and almost always powered by sail alone. Ships, like the one shown here, carrying precious metals, risked attack. Pirates were still active in the Ionian Sea, and sometimes slipped past the watchful eyes of the Athenian fleet.

# Mining and Money

For a long time, the Greeks knew nothing about money. They used a system of barter, exchanging a set of armor for two oxen, or even a woman for three donkeys. In the seventh century B.C. they began to use a curious type of currency, an iron spit or skewer, called an *obol*. (*Drachma* means "bundle of spits.") Eventually they discovered that it was more convenient to use coins, which they made first in silver and then in gold.

The Athenians worked the mines at Laurion, extracting silver from the lead ore to mint drachmas, which weighed 4.36 grams of silver. The mine owners employed slaves armed with picks to work in the low galleries and caverns.

Drachmas had a portrait of Athena, goddess of Athens, on one side and on the other her sacred bird, the owl. The coins were called *attic owls*. Other coins could be found in the markets—the Aegina *tortoise* and the Cyzicus *tunny*. These coins were made not of silver but of electrum, an alloy of silver and gold. Abroad, other coins were used like the Persian *daric,* with a picture of a bowman; it was made of pure gold. The Greeks obtained gold from the Black Sea coast, Andalusia, Egypt, Cyrenaica, and from all over the East.

A large number of metal smelters and smiths gathered at the port of Piraeus, where the merchant ships brought in cargoes of mineral ore from all over the Mediterranean. There was tin from Phocaea and Spain, and copper from Spain and Cyprus. The ore was refined and finely ground before being loaded onto the ships. In Cyprus the copper was melted, which took twelve hours at over 1000°C. Then it was made into sheets which could be carried on muleback. The sheets were then refined in clay kilns at intense heat, in order to remove any impurities. The copper produced was almost completely pure. But the Greek Cypriots, like all metalworkers, kept their manufacturing methods a close secret.

The Greeks discovered and mined most of the known metals, as well as mineral coal from the Black Sea, near Heraclea.

Slaves carrying metal ore in baskets. A winch carries it up to the surface to be treated.

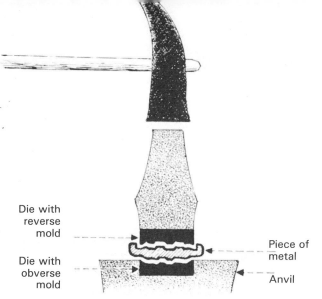

Die with reverse mold — Piece of metal

Die with obverse mold — Anvil

Coin making: A piece of metal was placed on an anvil between two dies or molds. The worker then struck out the coin by hitting hard with a metal hammer. The edges were then trimmed off. The Athens Mint stood to the southeast of the main square, the Agora.

Greek coins were made by hand in special workshops. From the seventh century B.C. on, electrum coins were made at Ephesus in Asia Minor, with pictures of bees. The first coins in mainland Greece were the Aegina tortoises, weighing over six grams of silver.

Fifth century coins from Greece and Magna Graecia (southern Italy). 1. Athenian tetradrachm, with portrait of Athena. 2. The reverse side, with the owl. 3. The tortoise of Aegina. 4. The barley ear of Lucania. 5. The bull of Gela. 6. The dolphin of Taranto. 7. The crab of Agrigentum (Sicily). 8. Athenian obol. 9. The quadriga of Syracuse. 10. Reverse of the quadriga with the nymph Arethusa and her dolphin. 11. The stork and tripod of Crotona.

Miners worked in cramped galleries, which were not very safe. They were airless, and props were hardly ever used. They were sometimes lit by clay oil lamps placed in the cracks of the rock walls. The miners had to work lying down, for the galleries were never more than three to four feet high. They used hammers, chisels, and picks. The ore which they worked so hard to extract was carried away in sacks. Working in the mines was the hardest sort of labor, and most of the miners were slaves.

# Wheat, Honey and Olives

In Greece there was a shortage of good farmland. As they could not grow enough wheat at home to feed themselves, the Greeks traveled abroad and founded far-off colonies. In the countryside of Attica there were few plains, and the farms were small.

In earlier times, in fact, there had been some big farms in Greece and large estates where people could hunt and raise cattle. But estates had been divided up by the system of inheritance; they became smaller and smaller and in the countryside around Athens they disappeared. The peasants there owned tiny patches of land which were not big enough to feed their families.

They made their own wooden-wheeled swing-plows. They had oxen to draw them if they could afford them, but more often they used donkeys or mules. Grain was threshed on a paved threshing-floor; mules were tied to a post and driven around and around to separate the grain from the chaff. Then the women crushed the grain in stone mortars to make flour, and from this the peasants baked their own bread. They only sold the surplus in the towns.

Families living near Athens went to the Agora, the great marketplace, to buy vegetables—cabbages, lentils, garlic, onions, and even melons and pumpkins, grown from seeds brought from Egypt. The women took flowers to sell, grown especially for religious and family festivals. It was also the women's job to spin sheeps' wool, and for a long time they wove the fabrics for clothes.

Peasants could make some money growing grapes and olives. They could get a good price for the strong wine of Attica, which was drunk diluted with water, and for olive oil, which they made in crude presses. Figs sold well, too, as did the honey from Hymettus, the only sweetener the Athenians had. The peasants knew how to attract bees and collect their honey by smoking out the hives. Those who could sell honey were lucky. It was much more profitable than breeding pigs or cattle, which were rare because of the shortage of pastureland in Attica.

Bee-keepers collecting honey on Mount Hymettus, near Athens.

Olives were picked by hand. If they were too high up on the tree to reach, the peasants used branches to knock them down. The whole family would join in the harvest, and the children enjoyed climbing in the trees.

In Homer's time, wheat was winnowed by throwing the ears into the wind so that the grain, which was heavier than the husks, fell to the ground. In the Attic countryside today they still use donkeys and mules for threshing.

Every autumn the harvest was celebrated, with special games in honor of Dionysus, god of wine and the vine. These young men, wearing wreaths of vine leaves, are trying to balance on oiled pigskins filled with wine.

Simple olive presses were made from oak or olive trunks. A heavy sackful of stones was hung from the beam, and the peasants pulled down on it. A block pressed down on the olives, which were heaped in a tub. The oil was collected in large earthenware jars.

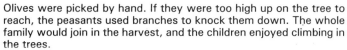

# Life in Fifth-Century Athens

Athens had a large population, although it was only a small city, measuring one mile from east to west. It was surrounded by a defensive wall, and within it the people were crowded into ten thousand houses, most of them occupied by single families. To the north lay the wealthy quarter, called the *Scambonidai;* here there were some beautiful stone houses with porticos. But most Athenian houses were small, huddled against each other, made of mud, wood, rough brick, and pebbles from river beds. They had skylights but no windows. As the town had a very poor water supply, they were provided with cisterns (public fountains).

The streets were winding, narrow, and dirty, and unlit at night. The main roads into the city were extremely narrow—it was difficult for two chariots to pass each other. The city had grown up, with no overall plan, at the foot of the Acropolis, the "high city." Built on a rock, the Acropolis was once the citadel of the Athenian kings. On it stood a collection of superb public and religious buildings.

In the lower city was the *Agora,* the public square and marketplace, which was the center of city life. It was crowded with huts made of beams and reeds, and the market resembled an Eastern bazaar. Plane trees grew there and at night they provided shelter for the homeless who slept outdoors.

Dirty water and garbage were thrown out into the gutters. Garbage was collected by gangs of slaves who were supervised to make sure they set it down a good distance from the city walls. Housewives did their cooking on braziers in the streets, where flies, fleas, mosquitos, and rats flourished in the filth. It is not surprising that during the time of Pericles thousands fell victim to the plague.

There was a striking contrast between the poverty of the ragged crowd in the popular districts and the harmonious lines of the great buildings on the Acropolis, with its many temples dedicated to the gods.

Women fetching water from a public fountain

In Athens the barbers were kept busy. Their clients were always men, who visited their booths to have their hair cut short. Some Greeks wore beards. Children wore their hair long until their teens. Slaves had their heads shaved.

Athenians bathed in public baths. If they wanted a tub to themselves they paid a fee to the man in charge. Water was limited and expensive to heat. They removed the dirt from their bodies with a scraper called a *strigil.* Afterwards they covered their bodies with oil.

Most Athenians rented their small houses. When they couldn't pay the rent the landlord would have the front door removed, and he might also remove the roof tiles or stop up the well. Tenants who couldn't pay joined the already swollen ranks of the homeless.

Bread had to be ready for mealtimes; it was served hot in booths. The baker would hire a flute-player to encourage the slaves as they ground the grain. And they were allowed to laugh and chat.

A thief is creeping into the inner courtyard of someone's home at night. He has gotten in by making a hole in the wall. Unfortunately for him, the noise has awakened the owner. The walls of Athenian houses were so badly built that it was easier for thieves to break

through them than to try to force locks. Thieves were called "wall-breakers." There was no real police force in Athens, so many thieves never got caught.

# Trading in the Agora

The Agora, the Athenian market square situated below the Acropolis, was crowded with traders' stalls. Partitions divided the shady streets into separate areas for each type of merchandise. As was the custom in Greece, the market was held in the open air.

The peasants of Attica came to sell their olive oil, fruit, and vegetables. Thebans arrived on mule-back from far-off Boeotia to sell the Athenians their delicious game, fowl, and fish, especially eels from Lake Copaïs. In the Agora you could also find people selling grain, garlic, and fruit. Butchers, bakers, and cheese-makers paid the city a fee for the right to sell their wares, and promised to give correct weights and measures—but they were often caught cheating. They often lost their profits by gambling away their drachmas at cockfights—not a good way to get rich! Slaves were also on sale in the Agora. They were sold at auction, and a laborer could cost around 200 drachmas. There were 300,000 slaves in Athens. Some were employed by private owners; others worked for the State, in civil service, or public works.

In Greek cities trade was well organized, for the livelihood of hundreds of thousands depended on it. The small Attic plains could not supply enough food for the 500,000 people of Athens, 200,000 of whom were the families of free men and metics (resident foreigners). So the food they needed had to be imported from faraway, and an eye had to be kept on provisions. A supply of wheat kept in storage at Piraeus had to meet the needs of the city. It was provided by merchants who were contracted to deliver grains to Athens from Egypt, Sicily, and the Black Sea.

In addition to barley and wheat, the merchants had to supply basic materials for industry. They brought vermilion from the Isle of Ceos to be used by dyers, wood from Thrace for the shipyards, and mineral ore and refined metal from all the colonies on the Mediterranean and Black Sea coasts. All these goods were unloaded at the busy port of Piraeus.

Oil sellers and a cock-fight in the Athenian Agora

There was only one source of light at home in the evenings—little clay lamps which burned oil, and stayed lit for hours on end. Potters made thousands of these lamps.

Weights and measures used in Athens: 1. Clay measures holding between 1 and ½ pint. 2. Brass weights marked with tortoises, weighing 127 grams. 3. Brass weight marked with a knucklebone, weighing 810 grams. The markings indicated the weight.

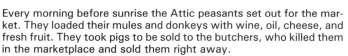

Every morning before sunrise the Attic peasants set out for the market. They loaded their mules and donkeys with wine, oil, cheese, and fresh fruit. They took pigs to be sold to the butchers, who killed them in the marketplace and sold them right away.

It could be difficult to decide between buying a hare from Boeotia or a nice fresh fish. In the market you could find huge tunny and sword-fish, as well as sardines and anchovies, which the Greeks were very fond of. Meat was scarce and very expensive.

Slaves were brought from Thrace, Asia Minor, and the Black Sea Coast. They were sold in the Agora once a month, at the time of the new moon. They were bought by families to do domestic work, and also by artisans.

# Crafts and Public Works

In Athens occupations passed from parent to child, whether you were a carter, carpenter, leatherworker, or sculptor. Knowledge was handed down in the family, and there was a system of apprenticeship to teach young people the secrets of their trade. In the towns there were many artisans. Free citizens kept the best paying and easiest jobs for themselves, leaving the rest to foreigners (metics) and slaves.

The State itself employed many workers in its public building programs. For decades, blacksmiths, carters, carpenters, and unskilled laborers were kept at work on the Acropolis and on building the two Long Walls running from Athens to Piraeus. There was always some kind of building work going on, and extra workers had to be brought in from outside. They began work at dawn when the cock crowed and finished at sunset. Unskilled laborers "rented out" their labor for a certain number of drachmas a day. They sang as they worked, and if there were a lot of them their master hired aulos players to help them work in rhythm. (An aulos was a kind of flute, similar to an oboe or clarinet.) Anyone who worked too slowly might be whipped

as a punishment. Workers were also punished if they were caught stealing. This could easily happen in bakeries, where it was very tempting to pocket the cakes!

In metalworking and pottery the work was hard. The potters could be found in the part of Athens known as the *Kerameikos,* or Potters' Quarter. They got their clay from the quarries at Cape Colias, six miles from the city. They mixed it with ochre or vermilion to color it yellow or red, and turned it on simple wheels. The molded articles were dried in the sun. They were decorated by hand by specialized painters. Only the most well-known signed their work. Everyday objects were made by smiths, carpenters, and weavers. Stonecutters obtained beautiful marble from Pentelicus in the Attic mountains; it was cut into blocks and carried down on wooden sleds.

Hauling a block of marble down from the Pentelicus quarries

Athenian women had their sandals made to measure. They would place each foot in turn on a wooden block and the sandalmaker would cut around it with a sharp knife. Women did not go to the same workshops as men, and they paid more to have softer leather.

A cabinetmaker used a drill and bow to bore a perfectly round hole in a piece of precious wood. The drill was kept in regular motion by the movement of the string. Artisans also had set squares and compasses to help them produce perfect work, including carved and in-

Metalworkers were highly skilled. They wore very few clothes, because of the heat in the shops. The metal was heated in kilns and the fires were kept going with goatskin bellows. The laminated metal sheets were then worked on an anvil, using hammers and tongs.

laid decorations. Good quality woods from Thrace and Asia Minor were used to make the chests, benches, and beds which were the pride of Athenian homes.

# Artists of Rare Talent

The 300 years from the sixth to the fourth centuries B.C. were a golden age for artists of all kinds. Painters and sculptors were in demand to decorate temples, sanctuaries, and public monuments as well as private houses. Art schools were founded, and their masters were highly respected.

In the fifth century B.C. there were many great sculptors, who are still famous today. There was Phidias, whose masterpieces included a gold and ivory statue of Zeus at Olympia, which has now vanished. Even better known was Praxiteles, who sculpted the Aphrodite of Cnidus. There was Callimachus, who invented the Corinthian capital and the clinging drapery on dancing figures. There was Cresilas, who has left us a portrait of Pericles. And then Scopas, who made a series of statues at Ephesus, with pathetically sad expressions. Today the works of these sculptors can be found in the great museums of the world.

Painters also had a very high reputation, though their work, painted on plaster and on wooden panels, has not survived. They used a technique called *encaustic,* by which colors were burned in.

Ceramic artists were just as highly regarded, and used to sign their work. They used a black varnish with an iron oxide base and a range of colors—white, yellow, purple, and blue. They illustrated historical scenes like the Siege of Troy and the adventures of Hercules, as well as hunting scenes and scenes of women's life. Painted jars and vases tell us much about daily life in Greece, as do the little statuettes made at Tanagra in Boeotia, which have been found in quantity around Thebes. They include portraits of schoolboys, street children playing knucklebones, and bakers making bread.

Other artisans contributed to the beauties of everyday life. Athenian jewelers made lovely necklaces, bracelets, and rings of silver and gold; bronze workers made hundreds of bronze jars and cups, and in Athens they invented mirror cases. Art was an important part of daily living.

A clay figurine factory at Tanagra

Different types of pottery. 1. Lecythus, used as funeral urn. 2. Pelike, amphora with swelling base. 3. Scyphos, drinking cup with handles. 4. Kylix, a drinking vessel. 5. Lecythus for perfume or oil. 6. Cantharus, drinking cup. 5. Oinochoe, wine jug. 8. Hydria, three-handled water-jar. 9. Stamnos, storage jar. 10. Amphora, used for storage. 11. Krater, bowl for mixing wine with water.

Phidias had help from other sculptors to complete his long frieze for the Parthenon temple. It portrayed the procession of the Panathenaea, a festival in honor of the goddess Athena.

Vases were dried in the sun and then painted. The earlier vases were decorated with black figures on a red base. Later, artists started dipping the whole base in liquid clay. The chemical reaction to firing in the kiln gave the vases a beautiful black glaze.

Statues were made in marble or bronze. Bronze statues were cast in a mold and when they were taken out they were carefully polished. Any little imperfections in the metal had to be filed away.

# Citizenship and Democracy

In the fifth century B.C. Athens had a population of about 500,000, 40,000 of whom were citizens. To be a true Athenian you had to have an Athenian mother and father. The city magistrates were granting rights of citizenship less and less freely. Although they welcomed foreign residents, called *metics,* they gave them a lower status. Metics were free to work and earn money, but they were not allowed to buy land and were excluded from political life, just as slaves were.

At an early age every Athenian was allocated to a particular administrative area called a *deme;* for example the urban deme of the Kerameikos or the rural deme of Marathon, on the Attic plain. The citizen carried the name of the deme all his life, and the head of the deme, the demarch (who was like a mayor today) had him written down on the list of citizens. When he was twenty and had completed two years of military training, he was allowed to vote.

For the city of Athens was a democracy, the direct government of the people by the people. The citizens met in a single Assembly, called the *Ecclesia;* they voted for laws and controlled the magistrates who were elected or appointed by lot to govern the city. The Assembly met on a hill called the Pnyx, and held up to 20,000 people. In fact though, only 6,000 had to be present to constitute a legal session. Citizens who participated in the work of the Assembly or took on the responsibilities of magistrates were paid a daily allowance.

The chief magistrates were elected for a year at a time. Nine of them, called *archons,* carried out civil duties and ten *strategoi,* or "generals", commanded the army and the fleet. The famous Pericles, who dominated Athenian politics for a large part of the fifth century, was never more than one of the ten elected generals. Any magistrate who lost the people's confidence could be made to leave the city by a procedure called *ostracism.* Sometimes they were exiled for ten years, simply because they had been suspected of ambition or tyranny.

An accused man, already in exile, is brought in a boat to appear before a special tribunal. His judges sit on the sandy shore.

Lots were drawn to appoint judges and assign them to particular courts. Bronze tokens with the names of the judges were inserted in the slots of an ingenious machine called a *cleroterion.* Black and white dice came out of the machine indicating the names of the judges.

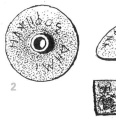

Every citizen was a member of the *Helaia,* the people's court of justice. Tokens were used for casting votes. 1. The disc with the hole filled in meant not guilty. 2. The disc with the hole left empty meant guilty. 3. Citizens who were members of the court carried a sort of identity card. 4. To vote for ostracism they wrote the victim's name on an *ostrakon,* a piece of broken pottery.

Any citizen had the right to speak in the Assembly. He would place a myrtle wreath on his head and was given a certain length of time. This was measured by the *clepsydra,* the water clock on the right. He was supposed to finish by the time all the water had run from one amphora into the other. A storm was a bad omen; it interrupted the Assembly's proceedings.

Sometimes Athenians preferred to chat under the trees of the Agora rather than attend to the city's business. They would be rounded up with ropes dipped in red paint; everyone could see who the late-comers were, and they had to pay a fine.

# Family Rituals

Men were expected to marry and have children, especially boys, to ensure that the family name would be passed on. When a young man was twenty, his father would choose a wife for him; the bride's father had to provide a dowry. The young couple would become engaged by a simple exchange of vows before witnesses, and then they could marry.

Weddings were usually held in winter, on a day when the moon was full. A wedding feast was held at the home of the bride's parents. Then the guests would form a procession and accompany the couple, seated in a mule cart, to their new home. The members of the procession would sing a chant to Hymen, god of marriage.

After the birth of a baby, the house had to be purified, and pitch was spread on the walls. Women were not obliged to keep their babies and could get rid of them, with their husband's consent. An unwanted baby might be "exposed," that is, left out in the open in a clay jar. But if the threshold of the parent's door was decorated with an olive branch, everyone knew that a boy had been born and would be accepted into the family. A woolen strip showed that the child was a girl.

Once a family had accepted the newborn child, the father could no longer get rid of it. He gave it his own father's name. In some towns, before recognizing his son, the father would dip the baby in icy water to make sure he was strong. In Sparta, babies were bathed in wine.

Family life centered on ancestor worship. The Athenians, like all other Greeks, had a duty to look after the aged members of their families until the very end. They believed that the gods punished families who failed to worship their ancestors at the altars at the entrance of their homes, where images of the dead were sometimes placed. On anniversaries the whole family would go to the cemetery to make sacrifices to the dead.

A wedding procession arrives at the bridegroom's house.

Children were cared for at home until the age of seven. They had pet animals and clay toys to play with. Babies were given their meals in baby chairs made of painted pottery. The best nurses came from Sparta.

Before her marriage the young bride (often no more than 14) dedicated her childhood toys and belongings to the gods. Then she purified herself by taking a bath in water from the fountain of Callirhoe, which was brought in a special jar, a *loutrophoros*.

When someone died, the body was washed and clothed in blue garments. Then it was wrapped with strips of cloth, placed in a shroud, and laid on a processional bed, with the face left uncovered. The head, wreathed with flowers, rested on a cushion. The family sur-

Between the fifth and seventh day after birth, the new baby was carried by its father or nurse around the fire, which symbolized the family. This was the family festival of *Amphidromia*. The baby was now recognized by its family and accepted at home.

rounded the dead person and hired mourners and lamented, dressed in mourning clothes. The body was buried, or cremated on a bonfire, before sunrise so that the gods would not be offended by the sight. If the body was cremated the ashes were put in a funeral urn.

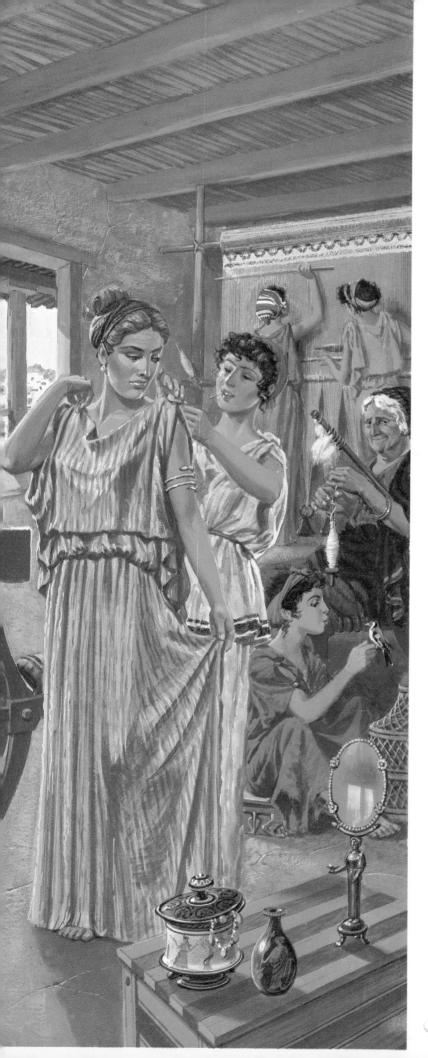

# Life at Home

Most Athenian homes were poor and had few comforts. There were no chimneys or running water. When people wanted to light a fire in winter they would remove one of the roof tiles with a pole, so that the smoke could escape through the hole. Only the houses of the wealthy had chimneys. The poor cooked their meals out in the street, and washed themselves at the public baths.

The fine houses in the wealthier districts were always two stories high. The rooms on the ground floor didn't open onto the street, but onto an inner courtyard surrounded by a colonnade. In these rooms banquets were held, friends were entertained, and the family met to eat their meals. Provisions were kept in a storeroom which was carefully locked. Only the mistress of the house had the key. The kitchen was next to the bathroom, which was warmed by heat from the ovens. On the first floor were the main bedroom and the women's apartments, the *gynecaeum*. The domestic slaves had their own small rooms in the house, too.

Houses were not usually decorated. The walls were whitened with lime, both inside and out. Only the richest people could afford paintings or mosaics to put in their living rooms, as well as tapestries, embroideries, and paneled ceilings. But since the Athenians spent much of their lives outdoors, they didn't have too many of these very costly decorations. They had a basic amount of furniture—chests for storing their clothes, chairs, stools, and tables. Their beds were made of webbing stretched across square wooden frames, with reed mats to serve as mattresses. In summer they slept outside on their terraces.

Women stayed indoors, where they supervised the housework and the care of the younger children. They were forbidden to go out alone, even to the market. Athenian women were subservient to the men. When husbands entertained friends at home, their wives didn't take part in the meal. They lived in the gynecaeum, where they entertained their female friends.

The mistress of the house in the gynecaeum.

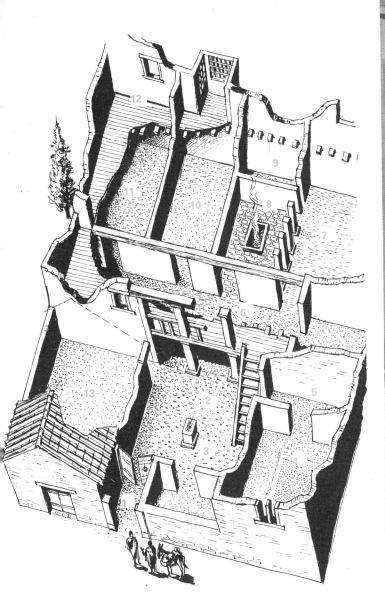

The ground floor of a large Greek house. 1. Entry porch and hall. 2. Courtyard. 3. Altar. 4. Dining room. 5. Pantry. 6. Colonnade. 7. Kitchen. 8. Oven or fire. 9. Bathroom. 10 and 11. Living rooms. 12. Part of the gynecaeum. 13. Workshop or storeroom.

Only poor women baked bread for their families. But wealthier women didn't mind turning their hands to cooking, if they wanted to make wheatcakes, for instance. The kitchen was a warm, bright, comfortable room. A tame weasel was kept to catch the mice.

Girls were brought up together and hardly ever saw boys before they got married. They only went out with their mothers. Their hair was worn long and they spent much time dressing it each morning. They washed in water fetched by slaves from the public fountains.

The mistress of the house would have her slaves weave wool. Blankets in beautiful colors were folded and stored in chests. People needed them in winter. There was no glass in the windows and it could be drafty.

# Grammatists, Doctors, and Philosophers

In the days of Pericles, every Athenian citizen learned to read and write, but the State played no part in their education. The city-state of Sparta had a different system. At the age of seven boys were sent to boarding school, where they were taught physical skills rather than mental ones. Spartans were brought up to be tough. Young boys and girls were both trained in strength and endurance.

Until he was seven, a wealthy Athenian boy was looked after by a nurse, who would tell him myths and legends and fables with morals about animals. Between the ages of seven and eighteen he was accompanied everywhere by a slave, a "pedagogue," who took him to school, heard his lessons and made sure he did his homework. He began school at seven; the schoolmaster, called a *grammatist* ("teacher of letters") taught him to read, write and count. He was paid by the boy's family. Later the boy went for lessons with a music master, which his parents also paid for. He learned to sing and play musical instruments, and also to recite epic poetry by poets like Homer. From the age of twelve he went to the *palestra* (a wrestling-school or gymnasium), to be instructed in sports and gymnastics under the direction of a trainer called a *pedotribe*. His education was then considered complete.

Anyone who wanted to learn more, and could afford it, could take lessons with the Sophists, who were traveling philosophers. They charged very high fees for teaching public speaking, logic, and debate. Young men living in Magna Graecia (southern Italy) could go to the university of the Pythagorians, who taught mathematics and philosophy.

It was a philosopher, Plato, who opened the first university in Athens, the Academy. Isocrates, an orator, founded a school of rhetoric where citizens could learn the art of public speaking. Doctors learned their medical skills in Asia Minor; the most famous of them all, Hippocrates, was born on the island of Cos. The army had their own doctors who ordered drugs from the Athenian pharmacists, who were skilled in using herbs for healing.

A young boy having a music lesson

The palestra was a sort of gymnasium where pupils were taught all kinds of sports, except running, which was practiced in a stadium. They took off their clothes and covered their bodies with olive oil to train. An instructor who was dressed in a red cloak and carried a forked stick supervised them. Older pupils taught the younger ones, and they all exercised to flute music. They learned all the sports known to the Greeks, from wrestling to throwing the javelin and discus. But only the richest learned horseback riding.

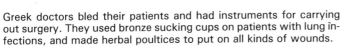

Children learned to write on wooden tablets coated with wax, using a pointed instrument called a *stylus.* The teacher first made them copy the alphabet, then syllables, and then whole words. People also wrote on papyrus, using split reeds as pens.

Greek doctors bled their patients and had instruments for carrying out surgery. They used bronze sucking cups on patients with lung infections, and made herbal poultices to put on all kinds of wounds.

Spartan girls trained in sports just like the boys. They learned how to throw the discus and javelin, and ran in foot races. Young Spartan girls were also taught how to dance and sing.

Famous philosophers went from town to town giving lessons. They were very well paid. Some of them, the Sophists, were extremely rich. Their favorite pupils accompanied them on their lecture tours all over Greece.

# Fun and Games

Men enjoyed getting together at banquets. There they were entertained by poetry recitals, accompanied by music on the cithara, lyre, and flute. They drank heavy wines, diluted beforehand with water and served in large bowls called kraters. Their wives were excluded from these feasts. But there were female dancers, who came in at the end of the meal to revive the flagging spirits of the diners. The guests often had to be carried home in the small hours, to the annoyance of their wives! Women had their own dinner parties, but they didn't drink as heavily as the men.

There was no lack of entertainment in the cities. In the markets you could see acrobats, jugglers, mimes, and puppeteers. The Greeks adored gambling, and enjoyed betting on animal fights. They trained cocks, feeding them on garlic and onion to make them more aggressive. Then they fixed metal spikes to their spurs and set them to fight each other to the death. They also arranged fights between dogs and cats. Men played dice and gambling games with coins.

In summer they liked to leave town to go hunting and fishing. They used dogs to drive rabbits into nets; they caught stags and boars by tethering a young lamb at the edge of a deep pit; and they caught partridges and quails in snares. Children caught small freshwater fish, using hooks and lines.

This Greek passion for leisure activities and games started at an early age. Children had a wide variety of toys, including clay dolls and noisy rattles. They played ball games and knucklebones together. They harnessed dogs to little carts, and taught themselves to carve wooden boats and build castles with potter's clay. The daughters of wealthy families even had dolls with jointed limbs.

Greek men enjoying the banquet.

Young Spartans had a very rigorous education. Their heads were shaved and they went barefoot. At the age of twelve the only clothing they had was a cloak for the coldest weather. They were deliberately kept hungry, so that they would learn to steal food in order to survive. In the middle of winter young boys bathed in icy water. When the countryside was covered in snow, they would rub their bodies vigorously all over and plunge into the Eurotas river.

Children's toys included the yo-yo, a double disc made of wood or pottery, worked with a string. They played a kind of hockey with curved sticks, and they had hoops, too.

Wildlife was scarce in the Attic countryside, and it wasn't easy to catch rabbits using a sling or bow and arrows. So dogs were specially trained to drive them into a net. The hunter then killed them with a club.

Young Greeks had tops and balls, they played hopscotch, and enjoyed swinging. Boys played a game with nuts: they piled them up in pyramids of three and aimed at them with a fourth. The winner took all the nuts. Girls played balancing games on see-saws made of planks and logs, and they taught themselves to juggle, using leather balls stuffed with bran.

# At The Greek Theater

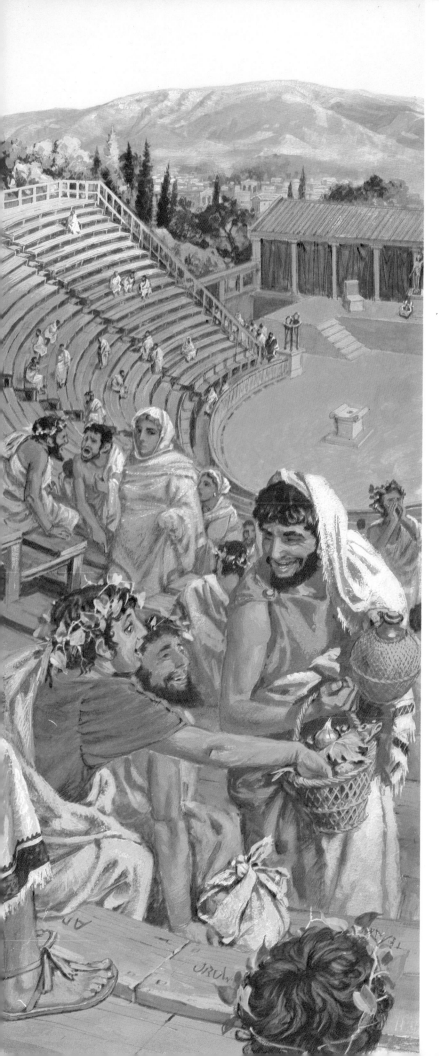

Greek theater was mainly a religious rite. At Athens there was an annual festival in honor of Dionysus, god of life, drunkenness, and creativity. It was called the City Dionysia, and included a four-day drama and poetry competition—during three days tragedies were performed, and comedies on the fourth. The richest Athenian citizens had to pay for the production of the plays. They were called *choregoi,* and it was their job to finance the productions.

Any *choregus* who failed to choose and stage a good play was in for trouble: the crowd would shout insults at him. But on the other hand, they applauded equally loudly if the show was good. A number of writers came from other Greek cities to take part in the competition. Those who had been selected were assigned a choregus who produced the play and hired a chorus master, flute players, chorus and actors. In 472 B.C. Pericles picked the great poet and dramatist Aeschylus whose play *The Persians* was produced that year.

The performances were attended by everyone in Athens—except for slaves. The audience included citizens, (the poorest were given free seats), young men, and metics. Sometimes citizens' wives came too; they sat together at the back.

Athenians would get up early in the morning to be sure of getting the best seats. The front rows were reserved for the magistrates, priests, and other high-ranking people of the city. The audiences brought food and drink with them, for you could spend a whole day at the theater and see four plays at a stretch, as well as dances and poetry recitals.

The actors were always male. They wore masks, and obeyed the principal actor, who was called the protagonist. Even in the comedies of Aristophanes the women's parts were played by men; since theater was a religious ceremony, women were excluded from taking part. After the performances were over the winning writer, choregus, and protagonist received their reward—a simple ivy wreath. But this was accompanied by enormous prestige and fame throughout Greece.

The public taking their places on the wooden seats of the open-air theater

Members of the comic chorus pretending to be horses. Wearing masks and tails they pranced round the orchestra (the dancing floor) to flute music, with others dressed as soldiers on their backs. Athenians loved this kind of dressing up.

From left to right: a tragic mask representing the character of Hercules; a comic actor; a comic mask; both sides of a lead token used as an entry ticket. Poor citizens didn't pay for their seats. The others were charged two obols.

In Pericles' day the Athenian theater was built of wood. But there were stone theaters all over Greece. In the center was the altar and the circular ''orchestra'' where the chorus stood. The actors performed on a raised stage, behind which were the dressing rooms.

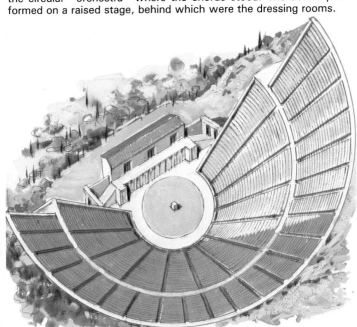

Masked actors performing the tragedy of *Oedipus Rex* by the great Sophocles. The old man with the stick is the diviner Tiresias, then come Oedipus and his mother Jocasta. The chorus stands behind an altar to Dionysus, at which the god was honored at the start of the play.

The Odeon was a small theater where poets and musicians were auditioned and musical competitions were held. Here a young cithara player is giving a concert to an audience of judges, singing verses he has composed himself.

# Sporting Events

Sporting competitions were encouraged by all the city-states and Greeks were trained from childhood to take part in them. Competitions were held in both the small towns and in the great sanctuaries—religious centers like Olympia and Delphi where crowds came to worship Zeus and Apollo.

A favorite sport was wrestling, which boys learned from the age of ten. People who liked violent sports enjoyed *pancratium,* a combination of wrestling and boxing in which every kind of blow was permitted except for putting out the eyes of one's adversary. The contestants rolled in the mud (the soil was freshly dug and sprinkled with water), and ferociously twisted each other's limbs. The fight was over when one of them lifted his arm to show he'd had enough. There were boxing matches, too; boxers wore strips of leather around their knuckles.

Children learned long jumping, and held stone or metal weights in their hands to help them adjust their arm movements. Throwing the discus and the javelin were also popular. Discuses could weigh up to eight and a half pounds. But the most popular event was the footrace held in a stadium. The track was usually about 200 yards long.

The festival of the Olympic Games was held every four years at Olympia, the sanctuary of Zeus in the Peloponnesus. Even slaves were allowed to attend, but not married women. The festivities attracted all the great men of Greece, and of course everyone who enjoyed gambling on horse races! The richest, like the general Alcibiades, owned stables which easily won the top prizes. In 416 B.C. he raced nine four-horse chariots at Olympia and carried away some splendid wreaths. At the end of the games, which lasted seven days, there was a solemn procession followed by a grand banquet where the results were announced. The names of the winners were celebrated throughout all of Greece, and they were considered to be heroes.

A chariot race

Two boxers in fierce combat, with a judge making sure that they follow the rules. Boxers wore leather bands around their fists and forearms, sometimes weighted with lead. Every blow was painful. The contest was over when one of them gave up or fell to the ground, exhausted.

Athletes always took a flask of oil and a sponge to the stadium. During exercise their oil-covered bodies would become coated with dust. They cleaned it off with a bronze scraper called a *strigil,* and then washed at the fountain.

Long jumpers, with weights in their hands, training in the stadium accompanied by flute music. The weights weighed up to ten pounds. At Crotona an athlete broke the record by jumping fifty-two and a half feet!

Six runners set off. They didn't start crouched with one knee on the ground, but waited for the signal leaning forward, with their feet together. The champion crowned with an olive wreath has just won the double-course, racing twice around the 200-yard track.

# The Importance of Architecture

Greek architects were talented all-around artists who put up temples dedicated to the gods throughout the country. The famous sculptor and architect Phidias, who worked in Athens under Pericles, was put in charge of the huge building projects on the Acropolis, where a number of magnificent marble temples were built. Phidias spent over 2,000 talents (12 million drachmas, or over four times the annual budget of the Athenian Confederacy), and employed a virtual army of quarrymen, marbleworkers, masons, painters, and sculptors. "It is in the interests of the people," said Pericles, "that I have created these great building projects, these works destined to keep a large number of industries busy for a long time."

Phidias designed the temple of the Parthenon, located on the highest point of the Acropolis, and dedicated to the goddess Athena. It was a masterpiece, built entirely in Pentelic marble. It took five architects fifteen years to complete (447 to 432 B.C.). Along the top ran a frieze 524 feet long, which includes sculptures of 400 human figures and 200 animals!

Athens built splendid monuments to the gods, and other cities vied to do the same, particularly in Sicily where huge temples were built at Agrigentum and Syracuse. Then there were the sanctuaries like Olympia and Delphi, with their temples to Zeus and Apollo. Places of lesser political importance, like Aegina, Argos, and Bassae (a small town in the Peloponnesus) even found the means to build superb temples.

The gods and goddesses, especially Athena, Apollo, and Zeus and his wife Hera, were believed to give their support to those who put so much time, effort, and money into glorifying them. No Greek would mind that thousands of drachmas were invested in the Parthenon, since they were spent not on the glory of Athens but on the good of humankind. For, it was said, no one who had set eyes on the statue of Zeus at Olympia could ever again be completely unhappy. The architects of Athens used their talents to improve people's lives.

A Doric temple being finished off. Workers are putting the final touches on the fluting and beginning to remove the tenons holding sections of the pillars together.

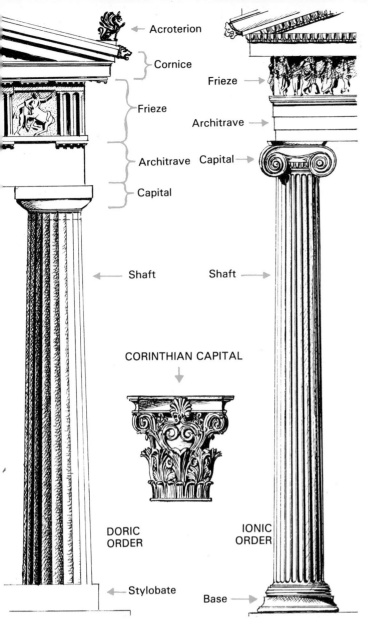

Acroterion

Cornice

Frieze

Frieze

Architrave

Architrave  Capital

Capital

Shaft   Shaft

CORINTHIAN CAPITAL

DORIC
ORDER

IONIC
ORDER

Stylobate

Base

Greek temples were built in two styles: the sturdy, simple Doric and the more graceful Ionic, with its scrolled capitals and slender fluting on the columns. The Corinthian capital with its acanthus leaves came into being after the Classical Age.

There was a long period of development between the very ancient buildings, like those excavated at Mycaenae and Tiryns, which consisted of huge stones piled up as if by giants, and the beautifully finished, perfectly smooth and polished walls of the Acropolis temples.

A winch was used to lift the marble blocks, carefully cut to size, and place them in position. They were then joined together with lead staples. When covered by the next row of blocks, the staples could no longer be seen.

To the left, different types of ''dressing'' for stone and marble. (1) Polygonal. (2) Rectangular isodomic. (3) Pseudoisodomic. (4) With headers and binders. Right; (5) Laconian tiles (6) Corinthian tiles, with antefix finishing off the roof edge (7) Antefix in painted terra cotta.

# Ready For War

Every Greek city-state treasured its independence and wanted to make sure the others respected it. This meant maintaining a permanent garrison of armed men. In the fourth century Thebes, for instance, had a "sacred batallion" of 300 soldiers, which was enough to make its enemies fear it.

Warfare was natural to the Greeks. It expressed the relationships between the city-states and the small rival cities. Athens, Thebes, and Sparta engaged in a lot of fighting. Every citizen between the ages of eighteen and sixty had to be prepared to be called up to fight at any time. Some of them were horsemen, but most were footsoldiers—heavy infantry called *hoplites*. Each hoplite was armed with a helmet and a metal cuirass (armor) to protect the body. These soldiers from Athens, Thebes, and Sparta defended their cities on the battlefield, first against the Persian invaders and later against each other.

The Spartan army had the strictest discipline of all. Between the ages of sixteen and twenty the young men went through intensive military training. When their training was complete they joined the army and stayed in for thirty years. They were unable to exercise their civilian rights or to even live a normal married life. They lived in camps, eating and sleeping with their comrades. Sparta had five regiments of hoplites. They were unrivaled in their maneuvering skills and their toughness in battle.

The Athenians also had a thorough training, but had less taste for the military life. They had other interests, like trade and commerce. All the same, Athens was a formidable enemy, particularly at sea. And the city still needed soldiers to defend it. So, all young men between eighteen and twenty (they were known as *ephebes*) had to undergo tough military training before joining the active army. In 431 B.C. this consisted of 13,000 hoplites and 1,000 horsemen. Until the age of fifty, they had to go to war if their country needed them. Athens had an army in keeping with its ambitions. In addition to the regular army, the city employed a large number of paid mercenaries.

An ephebe saying goodbye to his family.

In Athens it was the custom for ephebes to make a vow in the temple of Aglauros, at the north end of the Acropolis. "I will not disgrace these sacred arms, and I will not desert the comrade beside me . . . I will defend both the State and our gods . . ."

At the end of a year's military service, ephebes were given their shields in the presence of the People's Assembly, gathered for the occasion in the theater of Athens. They were also given a spear, and then passed in review by the generals commanding the armies.

Ephebes had already learned to throw the javelin during their school days; it was one of the skills taught in the gymnasium by the pedotribe. During military service they were taught to aim with force and precision, and to use spears in defence against cavalry attacks. They lived in garrisons in the forts around Athens, and went on marches through Attica under the charge of their officers. Military service lasted two years. Then the young men went home but could be summoned every year for a campaign if they were needed.

Due to the shortage of grassland there were not many horses in Greece, so the cavalry was small. At its peak, Athens had only 1,000 horsemen. Horses were imported from Macedonia, where there were plenty of spirited steeds. Even the footsoldiers, the hoplites, learned to ride during their military service. The young men from the richest families served in the cavalry. They had to pay for the trappings and upkeep of their mounts.

# Military Techniques

To win a battle armies had to strike swiftly and force-fully, beginning with a spear attack followed up by one-on-one sword fighting.

The Athenians, Spartans, and Thebans had the strongest armies in Greece. Their most vital weapons were not their cavalry or war machines, but the arms and legs of their footsoldiers—the hoplites. In fact, the cavalry's main functions were to carry out scouting duties and to pursue the enemy once they were in flight.

Hoplites carried short two-edged swords. They wore helmets to protect their heads, bronze armor around their chests, and metal greaves to protect their legs. They carried ash-wood spears, about six feet long with metal points. Overall responsibility for the army was held by a chief magistrate called a *polemarch*. The army was commanded by a general called the *strategos* who was elected by the people. In Athens, ten generals were elected, but usually only three went into battle.

The Athenians also had lighter infantry units, which included the peltasts, who carried javelins and wicker shields; slingers, who could throw stones or lead and bronze balls with accuracy a distance of 200 yards; and archers, who wore pointed hoods and also served as orderlies to the hoplites. The archers were often from Crete, and could fight on horseback. (The Scythian archers who kept order in the city of Athens acted as policemen rather than soldiers.)

It was not until later that the Greeks built great siege engines, so fortresses were hard to capture. They had to resort to besieging them, hoping to starve the enemy in the fortress into surrendering, or that a traitor could be persuaded to open a gate.

Strategy and tactics changed when the Thebans, followed by the Macedonians, created their celebrated phalanxes, massed bodies of spearsmen who would attack as one man, driving through everything and everyone in their way. But that was not until the fourth century B.C.

Hoplites being drilled. They are performing a wheeling maneuver, changing from column order to combat order.

42

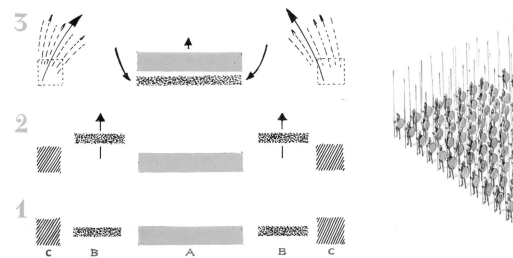

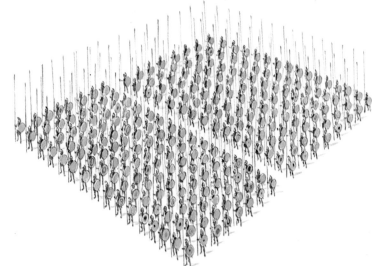

(1) The army's battle order comprised: (A) the heavy infantry of hoplites in the center, (B) the light infantry at the wings and (C) the cavalry outside. (2) and (3): In earlier times the light infantry advanced first and threw their spears, then moved behind the hoplites who attacked next, under the protection of the cavalry.

The Macedonian phalanx was subdivided into units made up of two groups of 128 footsoldiers each. As a rule hoplites stood a yard apart. When the officer, the *taxiarch,* gave the signal for combat, a trumpet was sounded and the men sang a paean, or war chant.

An orderly helping a hoplite put on his armor, watched by an archer in barbarian costume who holds a traditional longbow. The two sides of the chest armor (the cuirass) were joined with hooks. Sometimes

hoplites attached a fringed leather apron to the bottom of their shields, to protect their legs. They fought barefoot. On marches they carried their shields on their shoulders, hooked onto their armor.

# On the Battlefield

War was sacred to the Greeks. They believed that wars were willed by the gods, who watched the outcome with great interest. Before declaring war, the Greeks always consulted the gods by means of oracles. A troop of Spartans once let themselves be riddled with arrows because they believed the gods had not given them permission to retaliate.

Wars were played out on battlefields. Each side took up its correct position opposite the enemy, and waited for the time of attack. The general in charge always took images of the gods and some of the city's sacred fire on campaigns. Whenever he thought it necessary he consulted diviners, who could see the future. There were times when armies had no doctors, but they always had diviners!

A battle could last several days, but most were finished during one long day of fighting. The massed infantry, in formation, would launch a vigorous attack on the enemy. If the enemy's battle order broke up, that meant they had lost and had to withdraw. The cavalry would chase after them, harrassing them as they re-

treated. If they took refuge in a city, it would be besieged; the crops around it were burned and the fruit and olive trees cut down, giving them little possible chance of survival. A captured town would be burned and its inhabitants massacred or taken into slavery. Any wounded were killed on the battlefield.

After a victory, the army buried its dead and let the enemy's survivors bury theirs. They tied the enemy's weapons to a tree trunk, and this trophy was dedicated to the gods. Trying to steal weapons from a trophy was regarded as sacrilege. Any other booty was offered to the gods, too. It was taken to join the contents of the Treasuries of the great sanctuaries at Delphi, Olympia, and Delos.

A Persian horseman pursues a wounded hoplite.

In the time of Alexander (the fourth century B.C.) the Persians were building efficient war machines. They fitted sharp blades to the axles of their chariot wheels, which could slice through the legs of footsoldiers. At first the Greeks, led by Alexander, were taken by surprise.

An army marching through the Greek mountains, burning in the summer sun, would suffer badly from heat. Footsoldiers, armed with pikes, guarded the baggage which was carried in the center of the troop. Donkeys and mules carried provisions and spare weapons.

But their archers responded quickly. They aimed at the charioteers, who wore no helmets or armor. Afterwards, the terrified horses were calmed down by grooms and orderlies.

When a town was captured even the enemy's sanctuaries were ransacked. The victors were not obligated to respect the losers' gods. After all, the gods had deserted their people during the battle! Women and even children were either massacred, or taken as slaves.

No Greek would dream of leaving his dead companions without graves. After a battle the survivors hunted carefully among all the fallen men, and removed their arms and armor before burying them. The Athenians built monuments to honor their dead.

# Warships

In the fifth century Athens had two hundred *triremes,* manned by over 40,000 oarsmen, deckhands, soldiers, and sailors. After the Persian War and the Battle of Marathon, fought in 490 B.C., the Athenian general, Themistocles, decided that the future of Athens lay in her sea defences. The city had to become the supreme naval power with no less than 400 triremes!

A trireme was a war galley about 130 feet long and sixteen to twenty feet in width, rowed by three banks of oarsmen—170 in all. Fixed to the prow was a sharp metal spike which was used as a ram to pierce the side of an enemy ship. Triremes were made of pinewood, except for the keel which was oak. They could be powered by sail, but only oarsmen could move them with the accuracy demanded by battle maneuvers.

Oarsmen were usually recruited from the poorest Athenian citizens but could also be metics or, less frequently, slaves. The outcome of a battle depended on the skill and discipline of these oarsmen. A flute was played as they pushed their heavy trireme towards the enemy, commanded by the *trierarch* and his officers.

Triremes belonged to the State, but they were equipped and maintained by wealthy citizens whom the generals appointed annually.

With her triremes Athens dominated the Aegean Sea for nearly a century, sending out expeditions as far as the Black Sea and far to the West. Triremes played an essential part in the Athenian's power, and enabled the city-state to found colonies in the east and west.

Like the army, the navy never attacked unless the gods approved, and after a victory naval trophies were offered up to them. Ships had magical eyes painted on their prows, to ward off bad luck. And when Athenian sailors fought near the city's shoreline, they were inspired by the sight of the golden helmet on Phidias' huge statue of Athena. As goddess of war, she carried her spear and watched over all battles.

A trireme rams an enemy galley.

Oarsmen sat in three banks on each side of the ship. The oars were of different lengths according to the height of the rower's seat; those used by the top bank were about ten feet long. A flute player marked time.

The crew returns to their trireme, carrying their oars and leather cushions to sit on. They were paid an average of one drachma per day while at sea.

At the port of Piraeus a rich Athenian discusses with a shipyard foreman the ship which the generals have asked him to build. He is seated on a bronze battering ram which is to go on the end of the ship's spike.

(1) An Athenian coin depicting a ship's prow. It was struck in 306 B.C. to commemorate a naval victory. (2) *Biremes* were boats with two banks of oarsmen, lighter than triremes; they were quite common. When not engaged in combat, they were easier to power by sail. (3) A trireme on the attack. Its sides were vulnerable. One of the objectives in a naval battle was to get alongside the enemy trireme and smash all the oars with one blow. Thus disarmed, the ship could be spiked without retaliating. This maneuver demanded great accuracy, and the helmsman had to be very skilled.

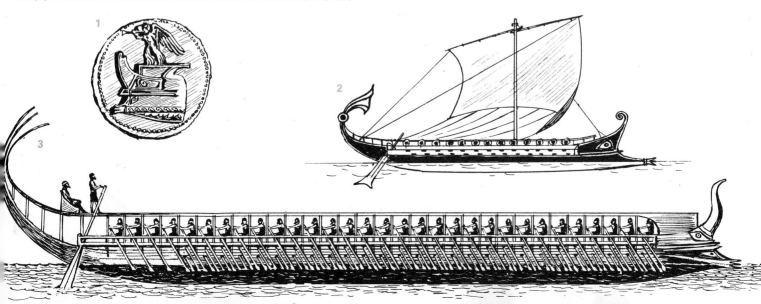

# The Power of the Gods

The Greek gods were everywhere—on land and sea, in the skies and the moon, in oaks and olives, in floods and earthquakes. Everything that happened was willed by the gods. Zeus sent thunder and rain, Aphrodite made people fall in love. Ares, god of war, granted victory or defeat. The sea god Poseidon, with his trident, made water gush from the rock of the Acropolis. The wheat that grew in Attica was the work of the earth goddess Demeter, who each year freed her daughter Persephone from her underground prison with Hades. If the sick recovered, they owed it to Apollo's son Aesculapius, who healed them in their sleep.

Greeks spent much of their time warding off bad fortune and giving thanks to the gods. They worshiped together in official rites in the cities. Offerings were brought to the altars of Athena, Zeus, and Apollo—libations of wine and milk; gifts of cakes and pastries; sacrifices of rams, goats, ewes, cows, bulls, and pigs. The animals chosen were white or light in color, and goddesses prefered female animals. Only Hades, god of the Underworld, liked black bulls. The victims were decorated with wreaths; if they had horns, these were gilded and garlanded with wool. Early in the morning the priest would slit their throats and their blood was sprinkled on the altar. A piece of their flesh was offered to the gods; the priests and those present ate the rest. Sometimes a sacrifice called a "holocaust" was made to the dead or the gods of the Underworld—the victim's body was burned without being eaten. If a god was very demanding, 100 bulls might be offered at one time; this was called a "hecatomb."

People about to fight on sea or land obviously needed the support of the gods. They used every means to find out beforehand what their future plans were, by divining. Divination, the art of foretelling the future, was practiced all the time. When a sacrifice was made the priests examined the victims' entrails for omens. Omens were also seen in the flight and song of birds, and dreams were interpreted. And at Delphi there was the Pythia, a priestess whose words were inspired by Apollo.

A goat is sacrificed to the goddess Artemis.

At Dodona, in Epirus in northwestern Greece, there was a temple to Zeus. In the groves around were sacred oaks, whose leaves delivered answers or decisions. The sound of the wind in the branches was interpreted by priestesses, who then gave practical advice to pilgrims.

Young girls placing a wreath on the statue of Hermes, messenger of the gods, in the street. There were statues of the gods on every street corner in Athens. Religious observances were followed at every moment of the day. An army never crossed a river without praying to the river god.

After a sacrifice everyone present was given a piece of the animal and ate it eagerly on the spot. The gods were believed to enjoy the aroma of burning flesh. The meat was always cooked, except at the secret ceremonies of the worshipers of Orpheus.

Water was scarce in Greece, and springs, rivers, and natural fountains were sacred. Springs were peopled by female divinities called nymphs. This peasant is purifying himself before crossing the stream in order not to offend the nymphs, who might take vengeance.

The sick made pilgrimages to Epidaurus, where they slept under the temple colonnades. During their sleep they would dream that the healing god Aesculapius touched the affected part of their body, and either healed them or gave instructions for their treatment.

A family meeting around a tomb on the anniversary of a death, to make offerings and libations. Woe to anyone who failed to honor their dead! Greek cemeteries lay outside the towns, and were always full of visitors.

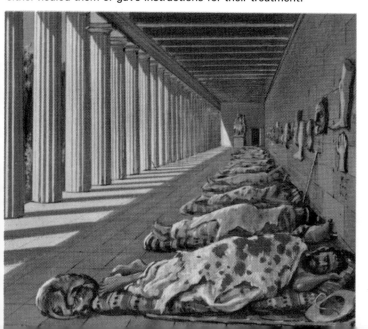

# Religious Festivals

In Athens religious festivals were held from one year's end to the next. There were ten months in the ordinary Greek year, and twelve in the religious year. Every month one god was honored by a festival which was usually a good excuse for merriment.

The year began in July with the great festival called the *Panathenaea,* which lasted for two days. Enough bulls were killed to feed the whole city. Every four years there was the Great Panathenaea, lasting four days. All the citizens, including metics, joined a huge procession in which young girls carried a specially woven *peplos* (a sleeveless robe) to present to the statue of Athena which stood in a temple called the *Erectheum.*

Next it was Apollo's turn. He was honored in October during the harvest festival. One of his gifts was a dish of beans. He was also celebrated in May, for as the chief god of purification it was his task to cleanse the city of pollution in the spring, and safeguard the new crops from pestilence and disease. But the most popular god was Dionysus; in both town and country Dionysian festivals celebrated the god of wine and the harvest for five days at the end of the winter. This was when the great drama and poetry competitions were held.

The Athenians looked to many other deities too. Women held their own solemn ceremonies in October for the goddess Demeter; no men were allowed at their feasts. They presented the goddess with sacrifices so that she would grant fertility to themselves and the earth. Poseidon, the bearded sea god, was worshiped in December; so were Chronos, father of Zeus, and his wife Rhea, who began the year by receiving the first fruits of the harvest.

The gods were always in people's thoughts, and they were always closely associated with human joys and fears. It was very important to keep them happy.

The Panathenaic procession at Athens. At the rear, the rich young men of the city arrive at the Acropolis on horseback. At the far left is the Erectheum, and to the right, the Parthenon.

The Great Dionysia. On the evening before, wreaths were awarded to the best drinkers—those men who had drunk their wine the fastest. The role of Dionysus is played here by a high-ranking Athenian magistrate, the archon ''king;'' his wife has been made queen of this curious carnival. The archon's chariot, shaped like a boat, is pulled by men dressed as satyrs in leopard skins and disheveled women called *maenads.*

Apollo was a god of purification. In the month of May two ugly men were chosen as scapegoats. They were beaten with fig branches and chased out of the city, with the idea that they took impurities with them. They were called *pharmacoi.*

On May 25 the city of Athens had to be purified. A procession carried an ancient olivewood statue of Athena to the harbor of Phalera. There they plunged it into the sea. Then they offered the goddess cakes and dried figs.

This is the Panathenaeaic festival. Citizens led four bulls and four sheep for the first sacrifice, holding olive branches in their hands. The procession gathered in the Kerameikos quarter and crossed through the whole city on its way to the Parthenon.

# Temples and Sanctuaries

The Greeks spent a great deal on the sumptuous temples they built in cities like Athens, Corinth, Argos, and Thebes, and in Asia Minor and Sicily. In Sicily the biggest was at Selinunte. It was 370 feet long and 177 feet wide, but it was never finished. From the seventh century B.C. temples were built of stone and often of marble. They were the wonder of travelers.

All temples were built to the same plan, around a large central hall (the *naos*) where the god's statue was placed, and an antechamber (the *pronaos*). All around were pillars holding up a sloping roof with a huge sculpted pediment. Architects made every effort to give them perfect proportions. The beautifully sculpted and painted decorations turned them into showplaces, which people came to admire from afar. The finest sculptures of the Greek world were in the frieze of the Parthenon and the statues in the temple of Zeus at Olympia.

When the Greeks gathered at the great sanctuaries they put aside their rivalries. Together they worshiped Apollo at Delphi and Delos, Zeus at Olympia, and Poseidon at Cape Mycale. They competed in generosity

to honor the gods with gifts of treasures. The Siphnian and Athenian Treasuries at Delphi were famous. And at Delphi the people of Naxos put up a column thirty feet high, with a sphinx on the top.

Games were held at Delphi, where the temple to Apollo was immensely rich. But the most famous games were held at Olympia. From 776 B.C. onward, the finest athletes from all over Greece gathered to compete for laurel wreaths at the Olympic Games. A Sacred Truce enabled athletes from enemy towns to travel safely through Greece. Anyone could take part in the games, so long as he belonged to the Greek world. Olympia thus symbolized Greek unity, centered on religious worship. People went to Delphi to learn the future of their cities, and to Epidaurus to be healed; but they gathered at Olympia simply to celebrate the fact that they were Greek.

The famous gold and ivory statue of
Zeus that was in the temple at Olympia.

The Pythia, Apollo's priestess at Delphi. Seated on a tripod in an underground chamber, she went into a trance (perhaps by chewing laurel leaves). Next door the priests waited for her to foretell the future, inspired by the god. Her answers usually had double meanings.

There were many visitors to Greek sanctuaries. Here a guide is describing the treasures which have been collected on the Sacred Way at Delphi. At the left is a bronze and gold tripod offered to Delphi from the booty captured from the Persians at the Battle of Platea.

Below left: Plan of a Doric temple in the Classical style. 1. *Peristyle.* 2. *Pronaos* (antechamber). 3. *Naos,* surrounded by an inner colonnade. 4. Statue of the god. 5. *Ophisthodomus,* or treasure room. Below right: The sanctuary at Delphi, built on the slopes of Mount Parnassus. Through it runs the Sacred Way (outlined in blue) leading

to Apollo's temple. Above the temple is a big stone theater. The sanctuary contained nearly 3,000 statues and votive offerings set out in the open. Some were sheltered under colonnades or in small shrines.

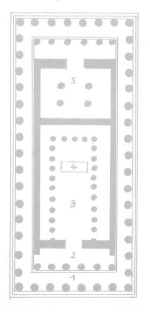

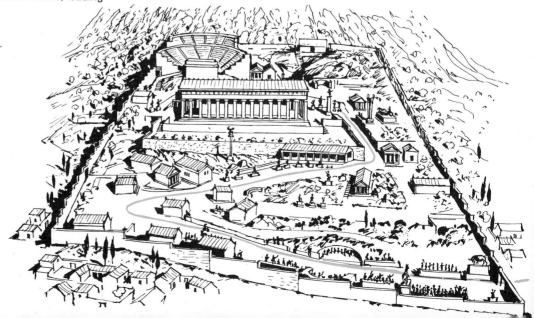

## Gods and Goddesses

1. Zeus, the supreme god. His symbols were the eagle and the thunderbolt.
2. Hera, wife of Zeus. Her sacred bird was the peacock; she decorated its tail with the all-seeing eyes of the giant, Argus.
3. Athena, goddess and protectress of Athens. She was born, fully armed, from the head of her father Zeus. She carried a spear and a shield with the head of Medusa.
4. Hermes, messenger of the gods, protector of travelers and dead souls, also the god of merchants. He was believed to have invented the alphabet and weights and measures.
5. Pan, the goat-footed god, healer and protector of shepherds and their flocks, for whom he invented the reed pipe, the *syrinx*.
6. Poseidon, god of the sea. He raised storms and calmed the waters with his trident.

7. Dionysus, son of Zeus and god of wine, drinking, and the arts.
8. Hephaistus, god of fire and metal-working, husband of Aphrodite. Another of Zeus's sons, he was lame and ugly.
9. Aphrodite, goddess of love and beauty, with her emblem, the dove.
10. Demeter, goddess of wheat and fertility. She holds a poppy, symbol of sleep and of the earth in winter.
11. Apollo, son of Zeus and god of harmony, light, music, and poetry.
12. Artemis, Apollo's twin sister, virgin goddess of the hunt, and responsible for sudden deaths. She never forgave an insult.
13. Hestia, sister of Zeus. She was guardian of the earth and the sacred altar flame.
14. Hades, god of the dead and the Underworld. His wife was Demeter's daughter Persephone. His door was guarded by Cerberus, a three-headed dog who prevented the living from entering and the dead from leaving.

# The Animals of Ancient Greece

*by Paul-Henry Plantain*

## An imaginary letter from Hippodamus of Corinth to his young nephew Kynophilus of Athens

. . . You tell me you'd like to write a book about animals, and ask me to give you any information I have gathered about them over the years. I am replying from Corinth, where Alexander, who has just been made Chief Commander of the Greeks, is about to cross the Hellespont against the Persians . . .[1]

## Wild Animals

You tell me you have seen the sculpted lions on the Terrace of the Lions at Delos. Over the last three centuries our sculptors have made many statues of this deadly beast, but it has not been seen in our provinces for a long time. Like the sphinx and the griffon, it is used as a symbol, as a fabulous guardian of our tombs. You may also have read the inscription underneath: "I am the strongest of wild beasts; I have taken my place on the dead man's tomb, and here I stand guard . . ."

The only fierce beasts left in our forests are wolves and bears. Just a few centuries ago there were large numbers of bears in Arcadia, in the heart of the Peloponnesus. There were few elsewhere, apart from Macedonia, Epirus, and Thessaly, particularly in the Pindus mountains.

They used to hunt lions by digging a deep pit with straight sides and covering it over with branches. At the bottom they put a lamb, and its bleating attracted carnivores. As a rule animals caught in this way were not killed; a cage was lowered to bring them out alive.

You have doubtless read what the historian and general Xenophon says about hunting. He considers it an important part of an ephebe's education, strengthening his body and preparing him

for war. Did you know that Xenophon actually hunted Helots, Spartan slaves, not long before you were born?

It's true that there is not much game in Attica. Of course there is plenty of foxes and birds—partridges, quails, larks, and thrushes; but to hunt boar, deer or the hare, you'd do better to go to Thessaly rather than stay around Athens.

1. We are in 334 B.C.
2. He means the European bison.

But I must mention that in Athens itself you can see an animal I am sure you have never encountered—a tiger, which has been donated to the city by some Syrian king whose name I can't remember. Among the other animals I can tell you about, there is one which apparently resembles a huge bull. Aristotle, who has visited Thrace, tells me he has seen several. He says, "These 'Bulls of Peonia' are completely covered in hair, with very hairy chests and legs."[2]

Rereading the history by Herodotus of Halicarnassus, who was a great traveler, I also found a mention of some very ugly animals called camels. They were used by the Persians, especially Cyrus when he vanquished Croesus of Lydia; it was camels who routed the Lydian cavalry—it seems the horses couldn't stand their smell. After Cyrus, Xerxes—whose fleet had been crushed by Themistocles at Salamis—

ROGER-VIOLLET

wanted to use them to carry his army's provisions. But on the way they were attacked by lions, and almost all were killed.

I recently heard that Alexander had learned that King Darius (whom he is preparing to attack) had elephants in his army, imported from India. He told Ptolemy[3] that if he is victorious he will bring some back to his Macedonian court. I must admit that I am very curious to see these beasts, which are said to be very fierce.

I nearly forgot to tell you a nice story I recently heard. Did you know that the young shepherds who take their flocks to graze on Mount Pindus have a charming way of honoring Aphrodite? In winter they go into the mountains and catch bear cubs, which they give to their ewes to suckle.

3. Alexander the Great's lieutenant

# Hunting and Hunting Dogs

BRITISH MUSEUM.

. . . I take up my letter again, having interrupted it to welcome my friend Lydias, from Athens. He came to return the money I had lent him, which gave me the opportunity to see him take from his purse some birds I haven't mentioned to you—"Laureot owls."[4] You'll agree that these are birds that one doesn't want to chase away! . . . While we're on the subject, I don't know whether you have had the chance to see the excellent Laconian dogs which Xenophon speaks of. They are the best dogs for rabbit-catching. I find it is much better to use dogs to drive the rabbits into nets, rather than trying to hit them with sticks as country people do. These dogs have slender ears and pointed muzzles. Aristotle says they are a cross between the dog and the fox. A true hunter should own this kind of dog, but he also needs to be skilled in using a sling or a bow for killing birds, in throwing spears at stags, and using a club and a hatchet should he encounter a bear or a wolf.

I have said nothing yet of fishing; it is a pastime unworthy of a free man, except perhaps when practiced in rivers, using a fly made of scraps of red wool, or in the sea using a trident. Fishing is really an occupation for those whose trade it is; they generally use nets to catch dolphins, tunny, and swordfish. On the Isle of Lesbos I saw fishermen leaving the harbor at night to catch fish with fireboats. They lit huge pinewood torches, and the fish, attracted by the light, leaped around the boat, making themselves easy targets for the fishermen's tridents. I don't particularly like fishing myself because it gives no opportunity for the healthy exercise of the body . . . But I do not despise a good fish dish.

4. Athenian coins which had the image of an owl on them, emblem of the goddess Athena; they were made of silver from the mines at Laurion.

# Animals and the Gods

Before saying more about animals in connection with the pleasures of the table, I would like, my dear Kynophilus, to remind you of the part they play in our dealings with Olympus.

Plutarch reminds us that "in foretelling the future, the most ancient and the largest part is the knowledge of birds . . . true instruments in the service of the gods." Did not Euripedes call them the messengers of the gods? Seeing an eagle, in particular, is a favorable or unfavorable omen, according to whether you see it on your right or your left. If you are in love, remember the influence that the wryneck may have on the heart of your beloved. This is the bird which Aphrodite tied to a wheel by its wings and legs, to further the love between Jason and Medea. If you want to question Apollo, don't forget to take him a goat. Before sacrificing it, the priest will sprinkle it with cold water. If this makes the bird tremble, it indicates that the god is willing to give you an answer.

When you make a sacrifice, you must always examine the victim's liver—a missing lobe is a serious omen. As you know, Cimon and Agesilaus were warned in this way of their forthcoming deaths.

If you go to Eleusis to worship Demeter, remember that if you want to be initiated into the Eleusinian Mysteries you must take a piglet with you. You must

take it along when you bathe in the sea; for both you and the piglet must be purified before it is sacrificed by the priests. Every god has his or her preference. Bulls are offered to Poseidon, cows to Athena, goats to Artemis and Aphrodite, cocks and hens to Aesculapius, and dogs, doves and horses to other gods. The victims must be healthy and unblemished. It is best to present females to goddesses and animals with light or white pelts to the Sky Gods, while the divinities of the Underworld demand victims of darker shades.

But beware of superstition, Kynophilus. My friend Theophrastus of Lesbos

has just written a book on the *Characters* of people today. In it he makes fun of those who fall into this particular trap. He says: *If a weasel crosses their path, they will not move until they have seen someone else pass by and thrown three pebbles in the air. Suppose they see a serpent in their house: if it is fat, they pray to Sabazios;*[5] *if it is a sacred serpent they build a shrine on the spot . . . If a bag of flour has been ransacked by a mouse they immediately ask a priest to interpret the event and tell them what to do next . . . If they hear an owl on their path they are afraid, and only continue on their way after pronouncing the formula: "May Athena take it away!" . . . Should they meet one of those garlic sellers to be found on street corners, they fetch the priestesses and ask them to purify them by dragging the corpse of a young dog around them in a circle . . .*[6]

As a historian I agree with Thucydides that one should place little faith in superstitious practices of this kind. I even question, I must confess, the truthfulness of oracles.

5. A foreign god of Thracian origin. One of his attributes was a serpent.

6. A rite in the worship of Hecate, goddess of witchcraft. She, too, came from Thrace.

The sacrifice of a pig

# Domestic Animals

Lydias has brought me a cat that he bought from an Egyptian merchant. He tells me it catches mice, but I have not yet seen it in action. Personally I am quite happy to trust my tame polecats to look after my grain. In some of our provinces, ephebes of your age entertain themselves by getting dogs and cats to fight each other while they hold them on leashes. They place bets on the fight and the winner's owner takes all the money. For my part, I prefer cockfights. I greatly admire the fighting spirit of these birds. They make a fine sight confronting each other in the ring, with bronze spikes shaped like pointed helmets attached to their spurs.

I would now like to turn, my dear Kynophilus, to the subject of animal raising as it is done in the country. If you wish to take up breeding yourself, do not throw yourself into it blindly. I would not recommend, for example, attempting to raise horses or cattle in Attica as the grazing land there is too poor. Better to settle in your country house in Thessaly for that, or go to Boeotia. Mules and donkeys, on the other hand, are content with poor pasturage. Don't laugh, Kynophilus—they can bring in a good income, for they are always in demand as beasts of burden and

for drawing plows. In fact, breeding mules is more difficult than you might imagine. As you know, they are the offspring of a donkey and a mare, and not every donkey wishes to mate with a mare. You have to choose the smallest mares, and remember that they are less willing to mate with donkeys when their manes are

long. According to Xenophon, this is why all mule breeders cut their mares' manes when they want to breed them with donkeys.

Pigs, on the other hand, are less profitable. Keep in mind that the suckling pigs that young men have to offer at the initiation rites at Eleusis only cost three drachmas each.[7] As for sheep and goats, not all our regions are suitable for them. Some cities, in fact, have decided to prohibit goat rearing because the goatherds take no care of them and let them wander about, trampling through cultivated fields.

I have tried keeping bees here, but their honey is far from having the flavor and aroma of the honey produced on Mount Hymettus. I think its quality must come from the delicate flowers of the heathland covering the mountain slopes. My hives are made of woven reeds and look like baskets. I have covered them with slats, and the bees attach their honeycombs to these. If you have the chance, reread Aristotle's *History of Animals,* which contains some excellent advice on bee-keeping.

Hippodamus

7. The same price as for a large fish.

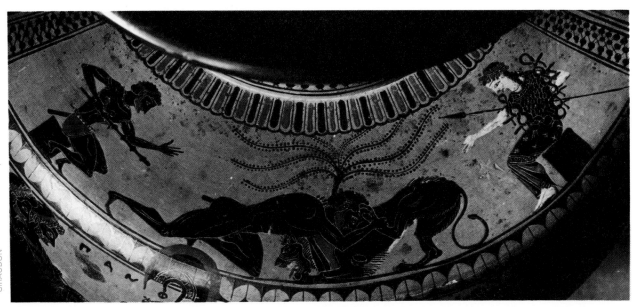

# Donkeys, Mules, and Horses

In Ancient Greece all overland transport had to be done with the help of donkeys or mules. Mules were also used for working in the fields and drawing plows, particularly in Attica where cattle were scarce because of the poor soil. Mules were also used for threshing wheat; they were driven around and around on the end of a rope attached to a post in the center of a cobbled threshing floor.

Although the artists of Ancient Greece have left us with many pictures of horses, horse breeding was not very advanced, again because of the scarcity of pastureland. In any case, Greek horses were not highly thought of—they were considered lazy and vicious. The Greeks themselves cannot be called natural horsemen. The cavalry under Pericles never amounted to more than a thousand men, and although his own mount was famous, Alexander the Great only lined up 700 horse soldiers at the Battle of Arbela in 331

B.C., alongside 40,000 foot soldiers. His own horse, Bucephalus, was brave and loyal, but no beauty if his name is anything to go by—it means "head of a bull."

Many works of art depict horses, but this is probably due to the fact that in the early days, horses were closely associated with Greek mythology. Later, of course, the Olympic Games, which started in the seventh century, included chariot races which were very popular.

There was no special breed of Greek horse and several different types could be found, mainly small Barbary horses. Only unneutered stallions were used for riding. Horsemen rode bareback with no stirrups, although spurs were sometimes used to urge one's mount over a ditch. Depending how sensitive the animal's mouth was different types of bits were used, either a "soft" bit, or a bit equipped with sharp edges.

Greek horses were not shod. So it was important for them to have thick, tough hooves which were supposed to "strike the earth like cymbals."

Horses were kept in stables with stone floors so that they would harden their hooves when they stamped. When they were traveling and the terrain became difficult, however, they were fitted with "hipposandals"—a kind of leather sandal or boot attached to the horse with straps. Finally—and this indicates clearly how low an opinion the Greeks had of their horses—it was recommended never to take out one's mount without putting a muzzle on him, "for the muzzle prevents him from biting and, since it goes around his mouth, it keeps him from wanting to play dirty tricks."

# Fish and Meat in Greek Meals

In towns, meat, other than pork, was expensive. People's basic nourishment consisted of fish, with bread, beans, pureed lentils, olives, garlic, onions and cheese. The fish markets were plentifully supplied with saltwater fish, particularly sardines, anchovies and tunny, shellfish and mollusks, cuttlefish and squid. But the Greeks enjoyed freshwater fish just as much, especially the famous eels from Lake Copais.

Meat mainly appeared on the tables of the rich, and of people who lived in the country. The main meats were pork, goat, mutton, fowl, and wild game. The main course was usually followed by a dessert which might include grapes, dried fruits, nuts, figs, and honey cakes.

Food was cooked in olive oil and very highly seasoned. The Spartans were famous for their "black broth," a kind of pork stew, very strongly spiced; its ingredients included blood and vinegar.

# Did You Know . . . ?

## The "song of the goat"

She goats symbolized lightning and he goats were ridden by Dionysus and Pan, who were both often pictured wearing goatskins. It is believed lieved that the word "tragedy" originally meant "song of the goat" and had its origins in a religious chant in honor of Dionysus.

## Domestic fowl

Cocks, hens, and ducks were found in plenty in back yards. There were guinea fowl, too, introduced from Africa in the fifth century B.C. According to Homer, Ulysses' wife Penelope owned geese.

Cocks were symbols of new life, watchfulness, and vitality; nevertheless they were sacrificed to Thanatos, god of death.

The Greeks also kept swans, which symbolized gracefulness and were dedicated to Aphrodite. Swans were believed to draw the chariot in which Apollo returned to Greece every year, after his legendary voyage to the Hyperboreans in the North. And Zeus took the form of a swan to woo the beautiful Leda; she produced two eggs from which were born the twins, Castor and Pollux.

## Grazing

The Greeks scarcely bothered to guard their flocks. Goats and sheep trampled all over the crops, and pigs lived semi-wild, finding their own food by rooting in the ground.

## Domestic animals

Cats were rare; the Greeks obtained them from Egypt. But in country houses you could find tame polecats, martens, and mongoose.

## Hera's birds

Peacocks became known in Greece in the time of Pericles. These beautiful birds were sacred to Hera, and they were kept around the goddess's temple on the island of Samos. Sultana birds, a kind of plump chicken with blue plumage and red beaks and claws, also lived on the lakes around her place of worship.

## Bull worship

The bull was a symbol of the reproductive forces of nature. In early times bulls were worshiped, but this changed as time went by. However, people continued to offer the animal as a sacrifice to the various gods of Olympus. In Classical Greece bullfights were held, in which horsemen tried to seize the bull by its horns and force it to the ground.

## Apollo's dog

Dogs also had an important place in Greek mythology. According to the legend, the first dog to be trained belonged to Apollo. He gave it to his sister Artemis, to take with her when she went hunting. At the time the ears and tails of dogs were not docked, as they sometimes are now. But a rich Athenian called Alcibiades decided one day to have his dog's tail cut short, in order to attract his fellow citizens' attention.

## Parasites

City streets and houses in Greece were far dirtier than you might expect. They were crawling with rats, flies, fleas, lice, and mosquitoes.

## Aphrodite's fish

Goldfish were sacred to Aphrodite, goddess of love, and they were very popular in Athens. So was an insect, the grasshopper, one of the symbols of music. Grasshoppers were kept in cages and some women put them in their headdresses, attached by golden threads.

# GLOSSARY

**Acropolis** The high, fortified part of Athens where the Parthenon was built

**Agora** The public square and market-place in ancient Athens

**Apprenticeship** A length of time spent learning a trade or craft. In return for being taught a trade the apprentice (person being trained) works for the employer for a certain length of time, often for no salary other than room and board

**Architecture** The science or art of building

**Armor** A protective covering for the body

**Chariot** A vehicle with two wheels pulled by horses used during ancient times in fighting, racing, and processions

**Choregus** (*pl* **choregoi**) A wealthy Greek citizen who paid the cost of putting on a play in a drama competition

**Cistern** A source of water, often a tank or public fountain

**Cithara** An ancient, stringed, musical instrument that was similar to a lyre

**Citizens** Those people who were allowed to participate in government and own land in a city-state. In ancient Athens you could only be a citizen if both your parents were citizens

**City-state** An independent Greek city and the surrounding territory with its own government and laws

**Colony** A settlement in one land ruled by the government of another country

**Demarch** The ruler of a deme

**Deme** A township in ancient Attica

**Democracy** A government that is run by the people

**Doric order** The simplest and oldest style of Greek architecture

**Ecclesia** A political assembly of Athenian citizens that met on the Pnyx

**Encaustic** A method used in painting and decorating to burn in colors by mixing them with wax and applying heat

**Ephebe** A young man who was undergoing military training

**Festival** A day or period of celebrating and feasting often to commemorate a great event or honor a god

**Galley** A warship powered by oars

**Grammatist** A teacher who taught reading, writing, and counting

**Gymnasium** First an exercise ground which later evolved into the place where philosophers held their open-air schools

**Gynecaeum** The women's quarters in a Greek home

**Hoplites** The heavily armed foot soldiers of ancient Greece

**Infantry** (1) Soldiers who have been specially trained, equipped and organized to fight on foot; (2) The part of an army made up of these soldiers

**Ionic order** A style of Greek architecture which featured scrolls on the capitals of the columns

**Kerameikos Quarter** Area in ancient Athens where potters had their workshops

**Knucklebones** A game like jacks but played with small bones

**Metic** A free, foreign resident of Athens who could work, but was not permitted to own land or participate in government

**Ostracism** The process by which ancient Greeks banished dangerous or unpopular citizens by a public vote on ballots made from potsherds or tiles

**Palaestra** A public place used by the ancient Greeks for physical exercise and training

**Pancratium** An athletic contest which combined boxing and wrestling

**Parthenon** The temple dedicated to Athena built on the Acropolis in Athens in about 447–438 B.C.

**Peasant** A farmer of the working class

**Peltast** An infantry soldier armed with a javelin and a crescent-shaped shield

**Phalanx** A special battle formation of Greek infantry made up of spearmen fighting in close ranks with their shields joined

**Philosopher** A person who studies the principles behind all knowledge and seeks the truth

**Pilgrimage** A journey to a sacred place, such as a shrine, as an act of devotion

**Pnyx** The hill in Athens where the Assembly met

**Sacrifice** To make an offering to a god

**Sanctuary** A place or a room where sacred things are kept

**Strigil** A scraper used to clean the skin after bathing or exercising

**Stylus** A pointed instrument used for writing on wax tablets

**Temple** A building where a god or goddess is worshipped

**Terra cotta** The reddish-brown earthenware which vases, small statues, and decorations on buildings were made from

**Treasury** A building or room in a sanctuary where money or valuables were kept

**Trireme** A galley with three banks of oars on each side, one on top of the other, used as a warship

# Index

Achaeans 5–6
Acropolis, the 16, 18, 20, 38, 41, 48
Aegean Sea 4, 5, 11, 46
Aegina 10, 13, 38
Aeschylus 6, 34
Aesculapius 48, 49, 59
Agora, Athenian 14, 16, 17–18
Alexander the Great 7, 45, 56, 57, 60
Animals 55–62
  domestic 29, 32, 57, 59, 62
  on farms 14, 60, 62
  sacrifices of 48–51, 58, 62
  wild 32–3, 56–7
Aphrodite 22, 48, 55, 57, 58, 62
Apollo 7, 36, 38, 48, 50, 51, 52, 53, 55, 58, 63
Architecture 6, 7, 38–9, 52–3
Archons 24, 42, 51
Argos 4, 5, 38, 52
Aristophanes 6, 34
Aristotle 6, 57, 59
Armies 6, 40–45, 60
Art 7, 22–3, 60
Artemis 7, 48, 55, 58, 62
Asia Minor 5, 6, 7, 13, 19, 21, 30, 52
Assembly, the 24–5, 41
Athena 12, 13, 38, 46, 48, 50, 51, 54, 58
Athens 4, 6, 10, 11, 56
  army of 6, 40–3
  building program in 38–9, 52
  festivals in 50–51
  fleet of 11, 40, 46–47
  life in 16–35
  population of 24
  theater at 34–5, 41
Attica 4, 5, 20, 56
  farming in 14, 18, 48, 59, 60

Banquets 28, 32
Baths, bathing 17, 27, 33, 37
Black Sea 5, 6, 10, 11, 12, 18, 19, 46
Boeotia 4, 18, 59

Cemeteries 7, 26, 49
Children 15, 22, 26–27, 30–31, 32–33, 36, 45
Citizenship 24–5, 40
City-states 6, 7, 40
Cock-fighting 18, 32, 59
Colonies 6, 14, 46
Cooking 16, 29, 61
Corinth 4, 10, 11
Corinthian capitals 22, 38
Crafts 20–21, 22
Crete 4, 5, 10
Cyprus 12

Death 26, 27, 44, 45, 49, 55
Delos 44, 52, 56
Delphi 7, 11, 36, 38, 44, 48, 52–53
Demeter 48, 50, 55, 58
Democracy 7, 24–5
Dionysus 15, 34–5, 50–51, 54, 62
Doctors 30–31
Dorian invasion 5–6
Doric order 38, 39, 53
Drama 7, 34–5

Education 30–31, 33
Egypt 5, 7, 10, 12, 14, 18, 59, 62
Eleusis 58, 59
Ephebes 6, 40–41, 56, 59
Epidaurus 4, 49, 52
Erectheum, the 50

Farming 14–15, 59, 60
Festivals 15, 23, 27, 34, 36, 50–51
Fish 11, 18, 19, 57, 61, 62
Fishing 11, 32, 57
Food and drink 4, 14–15, 18–19, 61
Furniture 21, 28

Gambling 18, 32, 59
Games 32–3, 36, 52, 60
Generals (strategoi) 6, 7, 24, 42, 46
Grammatists 30
Gynecaeum, the 28–9

Hades 48, 55
Hephaistus 55
Hera 38, 54, 62
Hermes 49, 54
Herodotus 57
Hippocrates 30
Homer 6, 30, 62
Hoplites 6, 40–43
Horsemen 6, 40–44, 60–61
Horses 11, 36, 40–41, 45, 60–61
Houses 16–17, 28–29
Hunting 32–3, 55, 56, 57

Ionic order 38
Italy, southern 6, 13, 30

Justice 7, 24–25

Kerameikos quarter 20, 24, 51

Macedonia 4, 7, 41, 42, 43, 47, 57
Magistrates 7, 24, 34, 42, 51
Magna Graecia 13, 30
Marathon 24
  Battle of 6, 7, 46
Marble 20, 23, 38–39, 52
Markets 14, 16, 18–19, 32
Marriage 26–27
Mathematicians 7
Merchants 10, 11, 18, 54
Metal, metal-working 10, 12–13, 18, 20–21, 23, 55
Metics 6, 18, 20, 24, 34
Military training 24, 40–41
Mines 12–13
Money 12–13, 47, 57
Mules 14, 15, 45, 59, 60
Music 30, 31, 32, 34, 35, 55
Mycaenae 4, 5, 39

Olives 14–15, 18–19
Olympia 4, 11, 22, 36, 38, 44, 52
Olympic Games 36, 52, 60
Olympus, Mount 4, 58, 62
Omens 25, 48, 58
Oracles 44, 48–49, 53
Ostracism 24, 25

Palestra 30–31
Pan 54, 62
Panathenaea 23, 50, 51
Parthenon, the 38, 50, 51
  Frieze of 23, 38, 52
Pedotribes 30, 41
Peloponnesian War 6, 7
Peloponnesus, the 4, 5, 11, 38, 56
Pericles 6, 22, 24, 34, 38, 60
Persephone 48, 55
Persians 6, 7, 40, 44, 45, 46, 53, 56, 57–58
Phidias 6, 22, 23, 38, 46
Philosophers 6, 7, 30–31
Phocaea, Phocaeans 6, 12
Pigs 14, 19, 58, 59
Piraeus 4, 5, 10, 12, 18, 20, 47
Plato 6, 30
Plutarch 58
Pnyx, the 24, 25
Poetry 7, 30, 32, 34, 55
Poseidon 48, 50, 52, 54, 58
Pottery 19, 20, 21–22
Praxiteles 6, 22
Purification 50, 51
Pythia, the 48, 53

Religion 5, 6, 7, 26, 27, 34, 35, 38, 41, 44, 45, 48–53, 54–5, 58, 62

Salamis, Battle of 6, 7, 57
Scopas 6, 22
Sculpture 6, 7, 22, 23, 38, 52, 56
Sicily 6, 13, 18, 38, 52
Sieges 42, 44
Slaves 7, 10, 12, 13, 17, 18, 20, 28, 29, 30, 34, 36, 46, 56
Sophists 30, 31
Sophocles 6, 35
Sparta, Spartans 4, 6, 7, 11, 26, 27, 40, 61
  army 40, 42, 44
  children 30–31, 33
Sports 30, 31, 36–7, 52

Temples 22, 23, 38–39, 52–53
Thebes, Thebans 4, 7, 18, 22, 38, 42, 52
Theophrastus 58
Themistocles 6, 46, 57
Thermopylae 4, 7
Thrace 4, 18, 19, 21, 57, 58
Tiryns 5, 39
Toys 32–33
Tragedy 6, 34–35, 62
Travel 4, 45, 60
  by sea 4, 5, 10–11
Triremes 10, 46–47

Water 16, 17, 28, 48, 9
Weights and measures 18–19, 54
Wheat 10, 14–15, 18, 48, 55
Wine 4, 14–15, 51
Women and girls 21, 26–27, 28–29, 32, 34, 36, 45, 50
  Spartan 31
Wrestling 36–37

Xenophon 56, 57, 59
Xerxes, king of Persia 6, 57

Zeus 36, 38, 48, 49, 50, 54, 55, 62
  statue of 22, 38, 52